THE
STARTUP STORY

AN ENTREPRENEUR'S JOURNEY
FROM IDEA TO EXIT

MARTIN WARNER

PEAKPOINT
— PRESS —

Peakpoint Press books may be purchased in bulk at special discounts for sales promotion, corporate gifts, fund-raising, or educational purposes. Special editions can also be created to specifications. For details, contact the Special Sales Department, Skyhorse Publishing, 307 West 36th Street, 11th Floor, New York, NY 10018 or info@skyhorsepublishing.com.

Peakpoint® and Peakpoint Press® are registered trademarks of Skyhorse Publishing, Inc.®, a Delaware corporation.

Visit our website at www.skyhorsepublishing.com.

10 9 8 7 6 5 4 3 2 1

Library of Congress Cataloging-in-Publication Data is available on file.

Cover design by David Ter-Avanesyan
Cover photo courtesy of Martin Warner

ISBN: 978-1-5107-7878-8
Ebook ISBN: 978-1-5107-7888-7

Printed in the United States of America

To my wife and kids, without whom this book would have been completed two years earlier.

CONTENTS

PREFACE

I hate turbulence. Who wants to fly through chaotic air currents where, despite the pilot's best efforts, the plane is plunging and soaring like you're riding a roller coaster?

I was born in England, but I live in the United States and I often fly across the Atlantic. But I reckon that if you want to be flung up and down in your seat you ought to be riding bareback at the rodeo. I dream of a smooth linear trajectory, cruising at speed through the atmosphere, without resistance, irresistible and fancy-free (and, of course, all-electric, but that is another story). It's funny how, even back on the ground, that so rarely happens. But somehow you still have to work out how to get to your destination in one piece, without crashing. And I've been helping would-be entrepreneurs do this for the last two decades. In a way, I guess you could sum it all up in the two words my old father would come out with when he was teaching me to drive and, specifically, how not to crunch the gears on an old manual car: be smooth! It's funny how the path is rarely as smooth as you might like it to be.

They say that those who can *do*; those who can't *teach*. But I wouldn't teach business unless I thought I could do it. I had already been running my classes and training programs for more than ten years when the following story starts. One thing I discovered is that theory is one thing, and practice, very often, is another. Which explains why this is a deconstructed reconstruction, a schizoid memoir, with my own experience straying a long way from the impersonal, omniscient musings of my more pedagogical self (a.k.a. the Professor, author of EntrepreneurSeminar.com and *The Entrepreneur's Book of Secrets*). The Professor doesn't have to worry about turbulence: He gets to see everything from on high, from a great distance, almost like he's standing on the moon and looking down on the earth through a telescope. Whereas I, in contrast, the entrepreneur in the field, having left the classroom behind, am trying to swim through a tsunami, and floating trees and assorted debris are smashing into me all the time, and I'm just trying to hang on and keep my head above water. The Professor is more cool, cosmic, and all-seeing; I am more on the verge of a nervous breakdown. He undoubtedly speaks with an English accent, a little like the Obi-Wan Kenobi of business ethics, with a lot of acronyms and checklists, whereas I curse and rant a lot more and sound as though I come from—and still live on—the mean streets of New York or New Jersey. Maybe we're both extremists, but stick us on the same page and you might have something like a balanced equation.

I'm still teaching, so I'm the first to admit that the history of bot-Objects is anything but a how-to manual. If anything, it's more a how-not-to; it ignores the Professor at nearly every turn. It's a risky experiment that takes place in the real world with dramatic consequences. But my startup story might stand as a user's guide to making it through, and finding the pot of gold at the end of a 3D rainbow, despite all the turbulence, beset by mishaps, missteps, bad ideas, bad actors, and near-failure, even through dark clouds of fear and anxiety. Sometimes you just have to throw caution to those godforsaken winds, take a deep breath, and fly by the seat of your pants. And finally, if the price is right, parachute out.

Some names have been changed to protect individual privacy (you know who you are!) and to give me a decent shot at not being sued.

THE PINK WHISTLE

In which we get straight down to business

I was mulling over the mysteries of color. People who are color-blind are basically right. There is no such thing as color. Humans invented the rainbow. Ask yourself, "What color are raindrops?" Our brains are (normally) wired to generate the effect of color out of random electromagnetic signals. All I needed to do, I realized, was reverse engineer the human brain. How hard could it be?

And then Tom O'Brien knocked on my door with a pink whistle in his hand.

At the time I was living in a farmhouse in Kent, in the south of England. It was one evening early in 2013, around eight o'clock. Tom is only a few years younger than me. And now he has grown a beard and spiky hair and looks like a proper grown-up. But back then he still looked like a fresh-faced boy to me, a particularly geeky kid (call him a technologist and an engineer—or mad inventor—if you will) who had been spending too much time locked away in his bedroom doing his homework, glued to his computer, or running weird experiments. Whatever he had been up to, young Frankenstein had driven a couple of hundred miles south from Nottingham to come and tell me about it.

"Hey M, I brought you something," he said, handing me the whistle. He liked to call me "M" because it made him feel like James Bond, or more likely Q, his techie sidekick.

We went into the kitchen so I could have a proper look at it in the light. "It's a whistle," I said. "Pink."

"Translucent electric magenta," he said.

"Pink," I said.

"With extra glitter. See the metallic particles?"

I poured us both a glass of wine. But I put down my glass and picked up the whistle and put it to my lips and blew. I was expecting a short, sharp note, like the sound of a football referee signaling the start of a game, but it was more like a mini-siren. It had a paddle inside it with slats like a watermill that kept the sound rolling.

"It works all right," I said. "But I can feel the surface is a bit rough. It needs smoothing down. You made this, didn't you? Did you make it using a 3D printer?"

He grinned. "I'm going to do a recorder next," he said. "Then the full orchestra."

Back then, personal 3D printers barely existed in the wider world. They were experimental. In a way, you could say that nearly all manufacturing machines are making something in 3D (if it's not a 2D drawing). But the quintessential 3D printer, conjuring up something or anything out of superimposed layers of a malleable substance, according to what instructions you fed in, was typically huge, the size of a mainframe computer. You could produce actual three-dimensional objects out of a printer. But only if you had a factory or an industrial design facility.

DIY fanatic that he is, Tom had built the 3D printer himself in his garage in a couple of weeks over Christmas, filching the software from open-source materials. "You built your own 3D printer? Why didn't you tell me?" I said.

"All you need is a good nozzle," he said, modestly. "And a few bits and bobs."

Demonstrably, Tom's invention worked. It was a Frankenstein's monster that could produce new objects. When Tom hit me with the pink (okay, translucent electric magenta!) whistle, I had a bundle of other ideas going around in my head. We had already worked on a number of different projects together, and we were supposed to be talking about a recruitment website and video interviewing. But probably because of my experience in producing and scripting and platforming films, I had also been thinking about different techniques for defining and generating full color. But until that point I had been looking for answers in the camera. Now I thought I could see the full color spectrum coming out of a nozzle. That was where it all started for me. Don't put it on the screen—make it real!

This idea blew all other thoughts out of my head.

So I turned the pink whistle around in my hand and considered the possibilities. "Can you do full color?"

"No," he said. "This was simply the color of the original filament I fed into the printer to produce the desired object at the other end." He took off his backpack and reached in and came up with two reels of filament of different colors. They looked like spaghetti. "I can do you blue and I can do you yellow."

"Do you mind if I chop off a bit of these?" I said.

I already had my Stanley knife out and sliced off a short length of each filament on the cutting board. Then I tossed both blue and yellow—like pieces of pasta—in a frying pan and lit the burner.

"You're going to kill your frying pan," Tom said.

"It'll be worth it," I said. "If it works."

I turned up the heat another notch. Soon the two filaments started melting. And as they melted so they merged with one another, the blue and the yellow pools pushing up against one another. I gave them a helping hand with a wooden spatula, shoving them around in the pan, impatient for them to cook. The smell wasn't too delicious, but my little kitchen concoction was starting to thicken up and bind, like a plastic omelet.

"Green!" Tom was impressed. And reassured.

"Shows it can be done," I said. "I didn't really know until I tried it. I mean, I know it works with light and paint, but I never tried it with plastic before."

It was, in its very preliminary, malodorous way, a proof of concept. Ever since I was a kid, I've been involved in reams of schemes and businesses of all kinds. And I was right then in the midst of steering a couple of different companies. Even so, the fact is you're always on the lookout for the next big idea to come along. I notice that the Professor devotes a whole seminar module to pontificating on "How to Find the Best Business Opportunities." But sometimes you don't have to find the best opportunities: they find you. You just have to be ready (I guess this is what the Professor means when he says "For so many reasons, we need open-mindedness").

And, just at that moment, the gooey, gunky gloop sitting in my frying pan on the burner in my kitchen looked to me like a glimpse of the future (even though the pan itself never recovered, and my dear American wife said I was an idiot).

2

TWO GUYS IN THE BATH

Branding

Actually, it wasn't a bath. It was, strictly speaking, a hot tub or spa or Jacuzzi. But I guess that counts as a very big bath with a lot of bubbles.

The hot tub was in my back garden, behind the garage, with a view over the hills in the distance. Since it was dark, you could only see a shadowy outline of woodland and the starry firmament above beaming down on us. The only terrestrial lights were the ones on in the house and the strip of waterproof LED lights around the edge of the tub. That and the glow that came from two mid-strength Cohiba Robusto cigars which we had lit up on our way outside.

But maybe darkness was good for the vision. Because Tom and I were seeing what could be, dreaming a concept into existence, while the bath bubbled away and we half-floated, weightless in the water, contemplating a whole new realm that had just opened up. And sipping champagne.

We felt we were at the beginning of something huge. It seemed to us then, as we gazed up at the universe, surfing a wave of

Havana-infused bubbles, that our 3D printer could be the next PC, as big as Microsoft or Apple. From the very beginning, we knew I was going to be CEO, Tom was CTO (Chief Technology Officer). He was a Steve Wozniak, the techie guy who would make it real, recruit the engineers and the manufacturer who could build it, and develop the website too. All I had to do was sell it to the world.

But first of all we had to work out what "it" was exactly.

"We need a name for it," I said.

"Like?"

"Well, it's got to sound serious, professional—so let's call it "Pro" something, like the MacBook Pro."

"Makes sense. You don't want 'amateur' in the name."

"It's got to be a desktop machine, obviously."

"But it doesn't fit on a desktop," said Tom, nervously. "It barely fits into my garage."

"OK," I said. "But it has to fit on a desktop in the home otherwise it's not going to sell to the masses. So put 'desktop' in the name. And it's a 3D printer. So that's easy—'Pro Desktop 3D.' Or shorten it to ProDesk3D? How does that sound?"

"Whose ProDesk3D? What are we doing? Who is 'we' exactly?" Tom was always asking the awkward questions.

We came up with the name of the company right there, sitting in the tub. It was obvious, really. Everyone was talking about "bots" in those days, because they wanted to be in on robotics. And weren't we making objects? We bounced it to and fro. We both liked the sound of "botObjects." We could worry about the small detail of hiring a crew further down the road.

Within about five or ten minutes of getting into the bath, we had come up with a name for the company and the product. I felt as though it already existed, even if purely at the level of imagination. We had started our startup right then and there, in the hot tub. I had this insane feeling—which owed something to the galaxies wheeling over our heads—that it was already written in the stars. We went on sitting there for the next hour or ninety minutes.

It's important to maintain a sense of realism. So says the Professor in Lesson 1. Maybe so, but a strong dose of madness, sky-high optimism, and a couple of Cuban cigars probably help too.

"The key thing is it has to be full color," I said.

"But 3D can't do full color," said Tom.

"Not yet. That's why ours has to do full color. It's our USP." I was recalling secret #32 from *The Entrepreneur's Book of Secrets*: "Find your USP (Unique Selling Point)." We had found it, hadn't we?

"Let me know how you're going to do that, won't you."

Trust Tom to quibble. He had this weird habit of worrying about practicalities. "Look at the world—that's full color. Just copy that!"

It turned out that one of the first things Tom had printed was a model car—balloon-powered—for his three-year old son. He had done it in red. The kid was knocked out by it, but his response was, "Thanks, Dad! Can you do me one in blue, please? I prefer blue. Blue is my favorite color." After an initial parental gasp of frustration, and contemplating his monochromatic creation, Tom had asked himself, "Why can't I do blue or green or purple or any other color I fancy at any time? If a 2D printer can do it why not a 3D printer?"

I let out a great cloud of highly scented, Havana-style smoke. We could worry about the details later. "And it has to look good too," I said. "It has to be a work of art. Tasteful. Classy. Comparable with Apple at least. Or Rolex. Or Nike Air. People have to want to own one. I want people keeping one in the box and selling it a few years later for ten times the price." We weren't the only 3D guys out there (not that we were out there, not at all, but you have to think ahead). So our hypothetical machine had to stand out. It had to be the most functional machine, but it had to have a beautiful form too. It had to be a Lamborghini or a Ferrari among 3D printers. Was that too much to ask?

When I thought about 3D printers, I realized one thing: we were at the beginning of the movement. People were just beginning to get excited about them. If you think of technology adoption in terms of a sine curve—or a wave—we were well past the phase of initial skepticism and we were fast approaching the peak (and, of course, were far away from contemplating any potential downside or "wipeout"). Everybody wanted to know more, to see if it was real. Now that I had seen—and blown—the pink whistle, I was a believer. Others would follow. All we needed to do was get on the ramp.

"How thick are your layers?" I asked. I knew that 3D printers worked using fused deposition modeling ("FDM" for short). In other words, they build up the object using thin layers of plastic, from the bottom up, one on top of another, like sheets of phyllo pastry (hence the phrase, "additive manufacturing"). Obviously, if you want a really fine finish, the thinner the layer, the better. The reason the pink whistle was so rough to the touch was that Tom had set up his machine to use relatively thick layers, around 100 microns, which produced ridges. The industry minimum at that time, so far as I knew, was around 50 microns. "Can we get it down to 25 microns?"

"Twenty-five? We can do that. But it's hard—a quantum leap down from 100 or even 50."

"You want to make a violin—or a cheese grater?"

"A violin?"

"Or even a golf club," I said. "It has to be smooth. It has to be streamlined. Nobody buys clunky."

"It's slower at 25."

"So let's speed it up!"

Lying there in the hot tub, borne up on a tide of bubbles like we were inside a giant bottle of champagne, we were convinced that there had to be a market for a fully functioning machine that did for 3D printing what Apple had done for mobile phones. Our machine would be different. Ours would be unique. The next generation. I scattered superlatives around like confetti.

So much for "realism." Sometimes realism sounds like a synonym for doing nothing. We were visionaries: our brains were racing way ahead of reality. We both had the attitude that anything is possible. We had already cracked open a bottle and smoked the cigars. We were committed. Maybe we should have *been* committed—to an asylum!

But so far all we had was a whistle.

3

FLY-FISHING

Deep background

Flying to New York, my head in the clouds, I had Tom on the seat next to me.

One thing you have to know about Tom: This is the guy who holds the UK record for "fly-casting"—how far you can cast your fly in fly-fishing. He even made and started selling his own flies at the age of eleven. He could build his own computers and code his own games by the age of thirteen. He dropped out of university after a year because he realized he already knew everything they were teaching him. He made a small fortune making and selling his brand of MP3 players (before the advent of the iPod wiped him out). If he could do all that he could surely conjure up the world's best domestic 3D printer—couldn't he?

I got my start in business at the age of eleven, finding my first customers in the school playground, and renting out games for the Atari console at £1 a night. Our headmaster, who didn't fully understand entrepreneurship, soon put a stop to that (having confiscated my games, he then handed them over to his own kids—I paid him back one day when I took his cane and snapped it in two).

Next it was cowboy belts. They were very popular at the time. I first came across them selling for £4 on a market stall in my hometown in Kent. You couldn't buy one in the shops for less than £15. I told my dad I want to buy up the whole stall. He was my angel investor: he funded a hundred belts. I sold them around local schools at £6.50 a time—I added on the 50 pence because it made it sound like more of a bargain. A profit of over 50 percent. After that they started calling me "Arthur Daley" in the playground—the shrewd but slightly dodgy secondhand car salesman, all-round wheeler-dealer and protagonist of *Minder*, a popular British TV series of the 1980s. I was still only twelve.

My other nickname growing up was "Rain Man" on account of my moody obsessiveness. My mother used to say that I was "autistic." I didn't really know what she meant by that. I took the Myers-Briggs personality test about five times, and for a while I thought I must be schizophrenic. It was only many years later that I was diagnosed as having a "hyperactive brain." Which sounds cool, and many people say to me "I wish I had a hyperactive brain." The reality is it's okay if you don't mind being awake at all hours of the night stewing over your latest scheme. I guess it's ideal if you're an entrepreneur or a chess player. (Fun fact: even now my wife says to people, "Don't worry, he's a little bit autistic" when I think I'm being as witty as hell. To be honest, with my social skills, it's amazing I even have a wife.) I learned chess around the age of five and dreamed of becoming the next Bobby Fischer. I never made grand master, but I think that's because I got distracted by the great and complex chess game that is business.

When I was a teenager, I naturally wanted to go to the Michael Jackson and Madonna gigs in London—the *Bad* tour and *Who's That Girl?* I was amazed by how expensive the tickets were. But I was even more fascinated by the price variation. You could find cheaper ones if you knew how. Back then there was no online option, so I just queued up. I bought tickets in bulk (using my profits from cowboy belts), held on to them, then sold them for double or triple nearer to the event. I started out in Soho, and within a couple of years I had built up a network of a couple of hundred "ticket brokers," a.k.a. "touts." They got their cut, but I made a small fortune.

Growing up, I was always a fan of Clint Eastwood in *Rawhide*. After that it was spaghetti westerns. Hooked on the silver screen, I had a notion of becoming an actor and went as far as studying acting in New York, but I didn't have really have the talent to pretend to be someone other than who I am. But still, I've always been a bit of a restless, rootless cowboy at heart. Which might help to explain how one day a few years back I found myself at La Défense in Paris, fifty or sixty stories up, standing on top of an AC unit with my nose pressed against the window and staring down at the world far below.

I had been working for a well-known investment bank—which, for the sake of argument, let's call P. J. Rogan—for almost a decade. I was like a gambler who had been given his dream job working in a casino. I started off as a trader, and I ended up designing risk metrics software that would do automatic trading and was far better at it than I ever was. I had turned IT management into a business (which we called "Titan"—to be distinguished from the *Titanic*) and was in Paris to finalize a deal with IBM.

I want to emphasize one thing—I wasn't about to jump: I'm not sure it was even physically possible to jump. Perhaps for fear that P. J. Rogan employees are particularly liable to jump in the event of a crash or a crisis, the windows in our building didn't easily open. I would probably have needed to smash my way out with a sledgehammer. But that was not my purpose in any case. If you've seen anyone jump out of a window you're less liable to jump yourself, I reckon. On the other hand, I did have this strange out-of-body sensation of floating out through the window and looking down from above on the insect-sized people far below. What was I doing with my life, where did I think I was going? I was, after all, one of tens of thousands working for P. J. Rogan. I was bringing in deals so big they couldn't afford to sack me. So far so good, you might say (as the guy hurtling down past the fifth-story window is supposed to say). But wasn't it also true, I thought to myself as I hovered out over the Place de La

Défense, that all we were ultimately doing was making more money for P. J. Rogan? So was that all I was, a moneymaking machine? Is that all my life is good for, multiplying money? And, what is worse—*for someone else*! Am I the parasite—or are they?

I've always had a sneaking admiration for people like Jordan Belfort, the Wolf of Wall Street, who can conjure up vast sums of money—and even for those like the Rogue Trader Nick Gleeson, who can cause equally astronomical sums to disappear. Either way there is something magical about it. But, in that moment of enlightenment and pseu-do-levitation in Paris I realized one thing: it wasn't about the money for me, or not any more it wasn't. I was tired of investment banking. Did any of it really matter? I had become a glorified software salesman, a heli-commuter, schmoozing corporate clients at Wimbledon and Le Mans. But my Wall Street dream was over. I needed to transcend my former self, to get out and create, I needed to build, I needed to make—something, it almost didn't matter what.

Maybe it was appropriate that I ended up, just a few years later, making something that could make anything (in theory). On the other hand, neither Tom nor I were exactly legends in the great realm of 3D printing. Not yet anyway.

4

FLYING TO NEW YORK

Trying out the tri-architecture

As I said, I hate turbulence. As a general rule, I won't get on a plane before checking the charts religiously for weather patterns. If I'm going to sit in a metal tube with wings traversing the ether, I want to know that it's going to be stable. And only then will I book the flight, typically the day before. Very often I will try to steer a pilot in the right direction and persuade them to adjust their flight plan to circumvent anything that looks like trouble. But for this particular flight I had no option but to get on it come what may. Hell or high water. We had to get to New York in a hurry. We had an exhibition to go to.

The best way to roll out a new business is to attend a trade conference or exhibition. And it so happened that there was a 3D printer exhibition, "Inside 3D Printing," taking place the week after we sat in the hot tub blowing smoke rings—in New York, at the Javits Convention Center on the Hudson River. We needed to be there: botObjects was about to take a bow. We had to talk to the industry, but more than that we wanted them to be talking about us. Admittedly, we were turning up at an exhibition with nothing to exhibit (on its own, the pink whistle would impress no one, alas). But there was also the sense that we needed to bestride the Atlantic right from the get-go and stick one foot in the door of the measureless American market.

Tom and I couldn't stop thinking about the new machine, still figuring it out, batting ideas to and fro, throwing out problems and then solving them on the fly. We had already established it had to have full color. But then a lot of other things followed on from that. I raised a glass or two to celebrate, like it was our birthday or something. Which in a way it was: We were exactly zero years old and we were already taking our first steps. Tom stuck to sparkling water because he needed to concentrate, he said. I was probably doing more of the talking, and he was doing the drawings, flipping over page after page of the pad on his knees.

Full color meant a bigger nozzle, with no less than six separate cartridges and six jets extruding thermoplastic and six different wires feeding into it. But then we needed more motors too: not two, but twelve. But if we needed extra motors, it was going to get hot so we would definitely need an extra fan at the back. "OK," says Tom. "So it's three fans now."

"Three fans. Doesn't sound very exciting, does it?" says I. Personally, I find champagne helps to concentrate the mind. I had one of my moments of inspiration. "Why don't we call it the tri-fan architecture?"

"How does that differ from three fans?" Tom didn't get it.

"It differs because we can patent it and it becomes part of the USP. How do you think Dyson got to be so big? I'll tell you—they have the greatest number of patent lawyers. No one can rip them off, not even China."

So now (says the Professor) we will introduce a key area of defensibility, and that is patenting. It's more applicable to businesses with products, because you can protect the design and utility (function) of a product. This is legal protection so competitors can't copy you. A patent lawyer will help you fill out the right application to ensure you have the correct jurisdictions for your patent.

Fast-forward to US patent office, one month later.

PATENT ATTORNEY: So, when you boil it right down, your so-called "tri-fan architecture" consists of three fans, one on top of another.
WARNER: It's never been seen before on the back of a 3D printer.
PATENT ATTORNEY: But in fact you're just adding one extra fan to the usual two fans, which you could call a bi-fan architecture.
WARNER: See how it's mounted higher up. We could change the layout perhaps. More of a triangle. That would emphasize the "tri," wouldn't it?
PATENT ATTORNEY [laughing his head off]: It's an extra fan, wherever you put it. You can't patent one more fan. There are a lot of fans in the world already. You're only about one hundred years too late to patent it.

Turns out maybe Tom the quibbler had a point after all (even if we would in fact end up with a hatful of patents). But the reality is that our tri-fan architecture caused a major ripple. The tri-fan acquired human fans, thousands of them. So to that extent I was right. And it gave us a bigger build envelope (the volume of space in which the object is to be created) too, which was crucial, even if it wasn't patented. At this point, flying to New York, my brain full of bubbles, I was convinced of one very big thing: everyone was going to need one of these. The 3D printer was going to be as indispensable an accessory as a phone or a laptop. It wasn't just for geeks. Every smart home would have one. Our printer, the botObjects ProDesk3D, was going to sit on every desk in the (promised) land. And if you didn't have a desk it could go on the kitchen table instead.

"Do you think we could put Amazon out of business?"

"Sure," said Tom. "I'm a bit worried about making it work though. 3D printers are notoriously flaky—they have this habit of breaking down."

"Think of it," said I, gazing into an imaginary crystal ball and refusing to countenance any of his qualms and queries. "With our printer all you need to do is press a button—no delivery time involved. No middleman. You won't have to buy anything anymore, just make it yourself at home." It was a beautiful, transcendent vision. Admittedly it might kill off Main Street for all time—make your own clothes, your shoes, your razor, your bed, and your bath. No more shopping. Everything would be DIY. Print your own house. Ultimately maybe we could make food too, feeding loaves and fish to the five thousand—like that scene in *Star Trek* where Captain Kirk presses a button in the galley and his lunch instantly materializes. It would be like a miracle. Our creations would be smooth and perfect and indistinguishable from anything you could buy in a shop or a showroom.

The history of 3D printing naturally inspired such reveries. It starts with the prophetic imaginings of sci-fi writers back in the fifties, conjured up in the pages of pulp magazines like *Fantastic Fiction* and *Astounding Science Fiction*. It is first described as a "molecular spray," so when a viable process was eventually devised in the eighties, it was a case of reality imitating art. From "stereolithography" to "selective laser sintering," from the "liquid metal recorder" to the "XYZ plotter," all these techniques had one thing in common: They got away from old-style industrial assembly. It was a postmodern style of production, where you went straight from a gleam in the eye of the beholder—or a CAD file on the beholder's laptop—to material, tangible simulacra, and simulations (as Jean Baudrillard would say), bypassing middleman and assembly line and factory. The dark satanic mills were no more. This was "Technology for Tomorrow," to cite the name of a conference I once organized at the Royal Albert Hall, back when I was known as a "futurist." 3D printing belonged quintessentially in the age of *The Matrix* and Industrial Light and Magic. It was pure science, but it looked like Hollywood hocus-pocus or the *Terminator 2* second-generation cyborg rising up mysteriously right out of the floor and turning into—well, anything you like: New and complex shapes that were way beyond anything clunky old traditional manufacturing could come up with. The 3D printer could, I realized with excitement, easily reproduce the mysterious black monolith beloved of Stanley Kubrick and Arthur C. Clarke, as featured in *2001: A Space Odyssey*, the perfectly geometrical con-coction of aliens so technologically advanced it seemed supernatural, metal but smooth and seamless, devoid of nuts and bolts and rivets and welding. (I was so taken up by the vision thing that I was tem-porarily forgetting the minor but significant detail that the printer itself would still need to be put together using more conventional means—and there, perhaps, lay the source of the rift between dream and potential nightmare.)

My brain was reeling with the possibilities. It wasn't just pink whistles anymore: pianos, guitars, handbags, bicycles, shoes, electric cars, space rockets, the pyramids of Egypt—there was no limit. (The pyramids, if you think about it, look like they were put together by an extremely large 3D printer with poor resolution; likewise, zig-gurats.) To my way of thinking, Jeff Bezos and Elon Musk were (or would be) toast. This was the new internet, bigger than big data—it wasn't just endless emails and flashy websites and simulated shop-ping; it could take anything virtual and turn it into something real. It wasn't meta—it was more magical than that. And all in your own home—a factory on your tabletop. It was the next biggest thing. It was huge.

Through the window we could see the glittering towers of Manhattan. Fortunately, this was one of those lucky days where tur-bulence had been minimal. The pilot had, weirdly enough, managed to find a route without my advice. I took this as a good omen. Not that it was going to be all plain sailing. Our brains, as we stumbled off the plane at JFK, were a swirling maelstrom of hazy hallucinations, brilliant theories, and crackpot schemes. No matter if there were a thousand problems, or a million. We knew we could overcome them all. Forget dotcom bubble; forget 2008 financial crash: think Apple, think Microsoft. If anyone could read our body language, it would be yelling, "We can do this! Don't tell me it's not possible!" Call it hubris if you will, the kind of pride that comes before a fall, but I don't know how you can start anything worth starting without this kind of mad overconfidence.

We set up headquarters at my house in Summit, New Jersey, and prepared to do battle. Our first objective was simple: SolidSmack, one of the tech industry's most astute media outlets. They were the gateway. We were going to change the world. We were going to print the world, on your desk. And they were going to tell the world.

5

THE GRAND ILLUSION

In which we meet the kid with the gun

By 2013, drawing largely on my own varied experience, I had already taught entrepreneurship to thousands of students over more than ten years. And I always tell them, in my professorial persona: "You have to be sequential, like a good builder, putting down solid foundations first. It's a pyramid. Don't start with the roof. Don't cut corners. Don't put the cart before the horse." And yet . . . we didn't even have a cart, and we sure couldn't wait for a horse. Maybe it was the effect of the plane or the champagne, but I felt we were already flying. And moving at light speed. Corners? Ha! Cut 'em! It was entrepreneurship on fast-forward—like an inverted pyramid.

"We are building a printer . . ." That was the way we put it. Which was true. We just didn't elaborate on exactly how much progress we had made until this point (nil). The present participle felt right—it wasn't done yet, but neither was it entirely in the future. After all, we had a man, a plan, and a fan (three of them, in fact). The basic rule is, you have to be able to weave a grand illusion—and yet still tell the truth. It's not a scam, but it is optimistic. We truly believed, so we weren't misleading anyone. It's like producing a movie. Producers sometimes get a bad rep on account of all their spiel. But the reality is you have to be able to talk a film into existence, right up to the point at which the cameras start turning—the first day of principal photography, as they say in the biz. Or, as the Professor puts it so neatly in his slightly cryptic way, "Focus on idea prioritization to align immediacy of actions." We had definitely prioritized the idea—and our actions were fairly immediate.

We had a story but we still needed someone to tell our story for us. I think it was Tom who found @solidsmack on Twitter after we tweeted out our existence and started boasting about how we were going to revolutionize the industry. Their tagline was "You make it, we cover it." They only had (then) about five thousand followers. But they were right on the money. They followed the 3D industry closely, and the industry followed them back. They were bloggers, pundits, obsessive reporters, always on the lookout for a design, engineering, or technology scoop, constantly tweeting about the latest developments. They were influencers who were followed by other influencers. "Yo, dude!" they tweeted back at us. "This is AWESOME!"

They would be our megaphone.

Walking into the Javits Center was like the crazy barroom scene in *Star Wars*. We were on Tatooine. Everyone was there, all eyeing up everyone else, scoping out the competition—all the weird inhabitants of the 3D space. Which is exactly where we needed to be. All it needed was some mad music. I was basically Han Solo and the ProDesk3D (with tri-fan architecture!) was my *Millennium Falcon*— the "fastest hunk of junk in the galaxy."

Naturally, the kid with the gun was there. This was the geek who had used a 3D printer to produce a handgun that worked. He even printed the bullets. The gun wasn't loaded at the time, and it looked kind of clunky, but I wasn't about to mess with anyone pointing it in my direction. I had no idea if it was legal or not. It may even be compulsory in Texas. Again, I wasn't about to get in an argument about it.

There were a lot of small vendors, but the big fish were all there. They included Hewlett-Packard and MakerBot and Stratasys and Riley Griffin, CEO of Mimetics3D, one of the major players, broad-shouldered with a broad smile and probably the world leader in the field (who would eventually call me). We all tipped our hats to the founder of 3D Systems, godfather of 3D printing and inventor of "stereolithography," the legendary Chuck Hull, a guy with more patents than you can shake a stick at (and who would eventually come to one of our demos). There were investors and there were journalists, all on the lookout for the next big thing. And, above all, the Javits Center was swarming with potential customers, thousands of them, roaming about and seemingly entranced by the treasures on offer in this 3D Aladdin's Cave.

The keynote was being given by Shapeways, who reckoned that people wouldn't want to own 3D printers, they would simply send an order to Shapeways to print it for them. But they would say that, wouldn't they? It was the exact opposite of our vision. We were going to push the quality up and bring the price down. And it was all going to happen in your own home. We were confident that watching a printer cook up a frying pan, for example, was way more fun than Netflix.

But, as I say, our main target was Arnie and SolidSmack. Unlike everyone else there, we had nothing tangible to show off. For all our fine talk of tri-fan architecture and full color and the like, we had no objective correlative, no actual working machine to speak of, beyond the DIY gadget in Tom's garage. Given our "focus on idea prioritization," some of the more nuts-and-bolts details were, of necessity, sketchy. We did at least have a website. Tom's team back in England had whipped it up the night before we hit the Javits Center. So we at least had a picture of the ProDesk3D—photoshopped. An artist's impression, shall we say. In orange (a color we borrowed from a laser printer). The dream was, in some sense, visible. It was almost real (technically, I guess you would have to admit it was about as real as the perfect girl/guy you've had tattooed onto your arm). We had even given it exact dimensions so we knew the desktop printer would actually fit on your desk. And we had a logo, with "bot" in orange and the "O" in "Objects" in the form of a drop.

That's all we were armed with when we bumped into our target at the Javits Center. SolidSmack consisted of a few guys, but it was mostly one guy, Arnie. His name was more of a nickname, acquired because he was absolutely nothing like Arnold Schwarzenegger. He was extremely tall, but rail thin, like a long-legged stick insect with a helmet of brown curly hair. We handed Arnie one of our business cards (which we had printed up at a Staples only the day before) and introduced ourselves. Our tweet had stirred people up and not everyone was a believer, but for some reason Arnie loved our (non-existent) printer. I guess it appealed to the geek in him. He, for one, was seduced by the tri-fan architecture and the Sputnik nozzle and the full color and the twenty-five microns. He (unlike the patent lawyer) agreed with us that our machine was a significant innovation. He saw us as pioneers, breaking new ground, reengineering the future.

The Professor, with his superior wisdom, once said that there are three kinds of ideas:

1. *Ones not worth pursuing.*
2. *Ideas worth consideration, but not ready to activate.*
3. *Those ideas worth implementing and well-timed.*

Arnie reckoned our idea was a definite 3. But, either way, note the emphasis on "idea"—at this stage that's all it was—a fantasy, a hypothesis, a thought experiment.

"What do you want to change?" he asked, pointing at one of the existing printers that were actually there, on show, the real ones that seemed so imperfect by comparison with the platonically ideal printer that we had squarely in front of our mind's eye. If we had had a tagline, it would have been: We Can Make It! But maybe it should have been: Fake It Till You Make It.

"Everything!" I snapped back. It was a slight exaggeration; ours was still a 3D printer, after all, just better than the competition. "And it's going to be twice as fast." The old printers took hours to print out the smallest object (and often went wrong). Ours was going to speed up the whole process. It was faster, smoother, and (of course) full color. Some of the old ones had a label stuck to them, marked "EXPERIMENTAL." Ours was the real deal (or would be). There may have been a certain amount of haziness around which tense to use: present or future or conditional.

Arnie thought the ProDesk3D was (or was going to be—same difference!) a marvel of microtech. Weirdly, not everyone agreed. Some people at the Javits Center thought it had to be a scam (to be precise, one online know-it-all commented, "total scam"). They started asking awkward questions like, When is it available? How many units? They thought we were full of bullshit and couldn't deliver on what we promised. And there was the Twitter backlash. "They're idiots!" was another blogger remark that sticks in the memory. "You've been had!" Some other bitter and deluded critic spat out, "We've been trying to do this for years—it's not possible!"

Were they right? Somewhere, amid all his more mystic prognostications, the Professor makes a basic commonsense point: "10) Ensure your product/service is ready for rollout. . . . The product or service must be ready for primetime and it must work." But we thought the temporary nonexistence of our product/service was a minor detail. He-who-knows-all even has a full-length "Readiness List." But why get pedantic about it? Ready or not here we come, was more my way of thinking. To infinity and beyond! Tom could sort out the details later. "Patents are pending," was our standard response to the skeptics.

Arnie promised us an online interview. We would have our chance to prove the doubters wrong. You can spend a ton of money on a good PR firm; or, better still, tell your own story; or, best of all, *be* the story. While we are at it, let us not forget the wise words of a certain Entrepreneur Seminarist: *The greater the amount of customers for the least amount of money spent is the goal.*

6

"IT'S UNBELIEVABLE!"

Faster than Michelangelo

"Are you sure we should be doing this podcast thing?" asked Tom. "We're going to put ourselves under a lot of pressure."

Podcasts were new back then. We were phoning in, and it was going out live to their dedicated listeners. Tom was already feeling the pressure. We had sold the idea to SolidSmack at the Javits Center. Now they were coming back at us with a full-scale interview. He wasn't sure we could carry it off. Wasn't there a danger we were going to make too many promises we couldn't deliver on? Weren't we going to sink before we could swim? Alarm bells were going off in my head too, but I tried to ignore them. I had a faint recollection of a heading in Obi-Wan's Entrepreneur Seminar: Determining Customer Optics and Avoiding Potential Risk in Product/Service Messaging. Tom was working on lining up a manufacturer, but so far we had nothing definite arranged. Unless you count the primitive cobbled-together monster in the garage (which would need the biggest desk in the world to count as a desktop), our printer still only existed as a collection of pixels.

"Keep the details vague," I said. "Don't be too specific."

"But I am specific," says Tom. "I'm a details kind of guy. That's what I do."

"Well, we need a few details, otherwise they won't have a hook they can hang their hat on. Don't worry about it, we can wing it. It's all about optics at this stage, trust me."

In the end, Tom agreed to do it, despite his understandable trepidation. We needed the momentum SolidSmack could give us. We took a lot of deep breaths and did the interview over Skype from my house in New Jersey. It went something like this . . .

ARNIE: Today we are speaking to Martin Warner and Tom O'Brien. They are, respectively, CEO and CTO, cofounders of botObjects, creators of the ProDesk3D printer, that threatens to revolutionize the 3D printing industry. Guys, tell us a bit about yourselves.

WARNER: Growing up I really wanted to be a movie star. Something like a cross between Brad Pitt and George Clooney. Or maybe Clint Eastwood. So I got into technology as a kind of safety net. But you know what, I love it now, and 3D printing is actually way more fun than films, because you can create real objects. On the other hand, if you're listening, Hollywood, I want you to know I'm still available.

O'BRIEN: My background is in hardware and software. I spend a lot of time coming up with bespoke solutions.

ARNIE: So tell us more about your ProDesk3D printer. What does it do?

WARNER: The clue is in the name. It sits on your desktop, but it's totally professional. It's going to be the first desktop 3D printer to offer true full-color printing. I tell you, it's unbelievable! In this space, coupled with our easy-to-use software, it can create anything you like. The only limit is your imagination.

[WARNER'S PROFESSORIAL CONSCIENCE: This is your conscience speaking: What easy-to-use software? You don't have the hardware, so how can you have the software? I'm just saying.

WARNER: Well, don't.

CONSCIENCE: *At the moment the only limit is your imagination. Especially the bit about Brad Pitt.*

WARNER: *Where's the conscience off button on this thing?]*

ARNIE: *How does it do color?*

O'BRIEN: *It uses what we call Fused Filament Fabrication, FFF. It can do five colors, a bit like the inkjet printer. And it's thermoplastic, it heats it up to 200 degrees centigrade, and it determines the rate of extrusion and what colors to mix in order to extrude the color of choice.*

ARNIE: *How does it compare to the other printers on the market?*

WARNER: *You know what they say about comparisons? They're odious. Or odorous. They make the other guys look bad. But, look, we're the only printer that does full color. And we're the only ones doing it in desktop. That changes everything. We're also three times as fast as any of our competitors. We're four times the resolution. And we have the tri-fan architecture. No one else has all that.*

O'BRIEN: *The industry standard is one hundred microns. We're at twenty-five microns.*

WARNER: *Less than the width of a human hair! Remember what Michelangelo said about how you make an elephant? You take a block of stone and remove from it everything that does not resemble an elephant. Well now you don't need a block of stone. You've got the ProDesk3D printer. So you can make your own elephant. It's a lot faster than Michelangelo too. How fast is it, Tom?*

O'BRIEN: *We can do 175 mm per second.*

[CONSCIENCE: *So, at that rate, to create an elephant, I estimate that would take approximately a week . . .*

WARNER: *But it could be a very small elephant—Michelangelo didn't specify!]*

WARNER: *There are different approaches to 3D. But the average consumer is going to say—I want to create the most versatile product—or objects!—and I'm going to want to do that fast, I'm going to want to do it in an accurate resolution, with a very smooth high-quality finish. And I'm going to want to use color. We can offer all that. Right there on your desktop. There is no limit.*

[CONSCIENCE: To your hogwash, you mean!

WARNER: Come on, we have a pink whistle, don't we? It works. So pipe down.]

ARNIE: Sounds great. But does it exist yet? Sometimes you use the present tense and sometimes the future tense. Which is it?

O'BRIEN: Of course we already have the prototype.

WARNER: We aim to deliver the first units to consumers this summer.

ARNIE: Is that like early summer or late summer? June, July, August, or . . . ?

WARNER: June. We don't want to keep anyone waiting any longer than we have to. We want our printer in the hands of the customer right away. They're going to love it. It's a whole new level of creativity.

O'BRIEN: It should be said, there are sometimes delays in manufacturing.

ARNIE: Just a couple of months from now! You're going to have customers queuing up.

WARNER: We certainly hope so.

ARNIE: And who is the target audience for your machine?

O'BRIEN: There's retail of course. Architects, designers. People who want to create something beautiful and do it in color. And the education sector could be huge. Color stimulates imagination among students.

WARNER: We don't want a target audience. A target is too narrow. Everyone. Anyone. You. Me. We have reinvented the 3D printer for the mass market. If you want to make something, it's for you. It's cheaper than going shopping. You know what they say—build it and they will come.

ARNIE: Price point?

O'BRIEN: We haven't determined that yet.

WARNER: It's going to be comparable to the price level of the existing machines. It'll be a Lamborghini but at a Mercedes price.

When we put the phone down, Tom spat out a single word: "June?" He had taken over from my conscience as the Grand Inquisitor.

"I know, I know," I said, with a definite feeling of guilty as charged. "But you feel like such a numbskull sitting there with nothing to say."

When they posted an article about it online a few days later, the headline read:

BotObjects Announce World's First Full-Color
3D Printer . . . for the Desktop

All of which was true: we had definitely announced it. We were one of "a few truly innovative products that stand out." They mentioned the thing about June too. To be honest, I did have some regrets about that interview. I could have toned it down a notch. Maybe "June" was a little overoptimistic. But they put me up against a wall. Of course I was going to have to come out with something. And there's nothing wrong with being a little bit late, so long as you catch the wave. Of course making that kind of commitment was a risk (as the Professor is the first to point out), but surely the bigger risk was missing out on our big chance.

This was the core sentence: "They announced the product today and, though we have yet to see a working version, if it works it will change 3D printing forever." I liked the line about changing 3D printing forever. I might have to use that one myself. But there was a big caveat. *If* it works. They were covering themselves. It was reasonable. They didn't want to take the heat if it didn't work.

"A full-color, plastic-printing, desktop 3D printer with self-leveling build platform and easy-to-use software—sounds too good to be true, right? We're hopeful this product is the real deal and we're looking forward to spinning up those motors when they push the printer out of production."[1] There must have been a lot of hopeful people out there, because the SolidSmack article—duly syndicated around the 3D printer world and beyond in home and lifestyle magazines—triggered a flood of customer inquiries. Preordering had begun. According to

---

1   Mings, Josh. "BotObjects Announce World's First Full-Color 3D Printer . . . for the Desktop." SolidSmack, April 26, 2013. solidsmack.com/fabrication/botobjects-announce-worlds-first-full-color-3d-printer-for-the-desktop/.

Google Analytics, we were getting one thousand live views at any one time—which over twenty-four hours translated to hundreds of thousands. Of course our website crashed, we hadn't expected to be so inundated so soon, and we had to migrate to a bigger server.

It was like we had accidentally tapped into a gusher. And it was just me and Tom in a hot tub. Our little not-yet-existent printer became the hottest story of 2013 in 3D. We had become almost famous, at least within the industry. "This must be what it feels like to be celebrities," as Tom said. Which was good and bad at the same time. To be clear, there were a few unbelievers who thought it was all pie in the sky. But generally people fell in love with us.

Some people fell out of love.

Some wanted our heads on a plate.

And then there were the ones who were jealous of us—the ProDesk3D haters.

Not to mention our very own fifth column—the mole.

7

THE PRENUP

Everybody needs downside protection

Flashback to when we first touched down in the United States, that lovely land of freedom and opportunity and unremitting creative destruction. To me the great symbol of New York is not the massed skyscrapers but rather all those the gaping holes in the ground where some earlier building deemed unsatisfactory has been torn down, leaving a promising tabula rasa, a vortex of possibility, before the next phallic monstrosity leaps up in its place.

Tom was impatient to whip his screwdriver out and get down to work. But the reality was that we were about to get hitched. We had fallen in love—with the project!—and we were hoping to stay that way. But we were going to be living and working in close proximity for the foreseeable. This was our honeymoon, a brief interval of sunny weather before the storm kicks in. Let's face it, even the best relationships can hit the buffers. So I thought we had better kick off with a list of do's and don'ts. We had to do everything right. By the book.

So I dragged Tom off to the nearest Starbucks.

"I didn't think you liked Starbucks," says he.

"I don't, particularly. That's not the point."

"What is the point?"

"It's symbolic. Do you know they started selling bags of freshly ground coffee? One outlet in Seattle. That's all. Bags. Beans. No cafés. No Christmas gingerbread pumpkin latte. No students sitting around all day long tapping away at their laptops. No old boys in the corner keeping out of the cold."

"No, I didn't know that."

I was a fan of Howard Schultz, longtime Starbucks CEO, and his memoir, *Pour Your Heart into It*. "Do you know how big Starbucks is now?"

"No."

"Neither do I. And that is the point. Nobody knows. It's huge. It's like the British Empire of old. The sun never sets on Starbucks. You can't walk a couple of blocks without bumping into one. That's what we want. We want to take over the world. One small step for a man, one giant leap for 3D printer technology."

Tom pondered my point. "So really we could have gone to McDonald's then?"

"Yes. But I only wanted a coffee. The coffee's better here. Eventually we will simply print a decaf cappuccino with oat milk while sitting at the desk."

"We will?"

I could tell Tom didn't really get the romance, the poetry of the whole thing. I was tying the knot with a guy who knew how to put up the shelves and fix the plumbing. But, then again, wandering lonely as a cloud only takes you so far.

"We have to follow the rules," I said.

"What are the rules?"

"The rules are the rules I've already set down in my Entrepreneur Seminar program."

"So they're basically your rules?"

I took a sip of my cappuccino. It was good. Schultz knew what he was doing, all that research in Italian cafés. "You could say that. But they're rules forged from a lot of experience—a lot of pain."

"Your bible."

"I don't want to use the word 'bible,' but it's like the Bible. Yeah, the business bible."

"The gospel according to Martin Warner."

Tom, I could tell, wasn't fully into the theory of entrepreneurship. "There are some things I'm religious about, it's true. Most of it is common sense. We have to minimize risk and maximize performance. Agreed?"

"Agreed."

"But we need downside protection."

"What is downside protection?"

For this one day, I was having to fully assume my professorial alter ego. "We are talking asset accretion, my boy." Sometimes Tom made me feel as old as Gandalf. "It's what you fall back on if it all goes down the chute."

"Got it," he said, nodding in a way that suggested that he was going to leave all the asset accretion to me.

I tried looking at it more from his point of view. I appreciated he had a big job on his hands. "We're doing something that hasn't been done before."

"Well . . ."

"I know there are other 3D printers out there! But this is the one, right? Full color, faster resolution, all that."

"Yeah, for sure."

"And it has to be pure art too."

"Art?" Tom was more about the science.

"It mustn't look plastic or shitty."

"It won't."

"People have to fall in love with it. We have to make it look so good they don't even care if it works or not. The ProDesk3D has to be something unique. Collectable. Like a Picasso or a Warhol. Also we can do a limited edition, like an Apple."

"Got it, got it."

"You know if those printers are not delivered, any money received is not recognized as revenue, don't you?"

"OK."

"That means you can't spend it!"

"Got it." Sometimes when Tom says "Got it" he seems to mean he's barely listening. I guess this whole rigmarole was useful for me, anyway, even if not for him. He was a serious geek, after all. He could make money, but he wouldn't have time to actually spend any. All the same, I thought I should try and get his attention.

"You know we are going to be facing some very vicious tactics from our adversaries."

"We have adversaries? We haven't started anything yet!" Tom was such an innocent in the ways of the world.

"Everyone is going to hate us."

"They are?"

"Think about it. We're disrupting the whole industry. Everything else is rubbish. Ours is better. Of course we are going to have enemies."

"I hadn't thought about that," says Tom.

"It's okay though," I said. "We're like the protagonist. And the protagonist needs antagonists, otherwise what's the point? Conflict is normal. It's a jungle, but we have razor-sharp teeth, we'll survive."

Tom breathed a sigh of relief. He wasn't really into conflict.

"The good news is that the conflict will be good publicity anyway. We won't have to pay an awful lot for PR. And of course we have to know the floor and the ceiling."

"Of course." He thought about it. "What is the floor?"

"The floor is basically bankruptcy. The whole thing goes under. It's basically the worst thing you can imagine."

"Do we go to jail too?"

"Maybe not. But we can't let any customers down. We have to deliver on our promises. If you're going to miss a deadline you'd better tell me."

"So what's the ceiling?"

I could tell Tom was starting to rethink the whole deal. Which was basically a good thing, but still I thought I could afford to dwell on the positive for a moment.

"The ceiling is billions. This could be a billion-dollar industry. If we get it right. We could be at the top of the tree."

He let out a whistle. "That sounds like a pretty high ceiling."

"The sky is the limit."

"I thought you were going to say that."

"No decision can be made without running it past both of us, right?"

"No problem." Tom didn't particularly want to make the decisions.

"It's no compromise from here on out," I said. "You can't just take your printer off the shelf."

"No compromise."

"We will never compromise, because the thing about Rome is it took a while to build but it can be razed in a few hours."

"It must have taken a bit longer than that surely. Wasn't Nero playing the violin and all?"

"Okay, forget fucking Rome! We will destroy our reputations and then we are toast."

He nodded wisely. "Toast, yeah. You know what, I could just fancy a bit of toast. Do you think they do any here?"

"We're going to be under a shitload of pressure all the time, no question about that. The market, the media—they're not going to give you time—or excuses."

"Hold on, I'm just going to get a croissant."

I waited till he sat himself down again and was stuffing his face. "They only had chocolate," he said.

"Why are we even doing this?" I said. "It's not as if we're going to go hungry, is it?"

He thought about it while dunking chocolate croissant in his cappuccino. "I'd like to make my mark. I want to solve the problem and show people we can do it."

Tom was so sincere about everything. I almost burst into tears at that line of his. He was a good guy to have on my side. I decided not to hit him with my "nodal approach to sales" or my theories about hiring and A-players and B-players. He could leave all that to me.

Perhaps I had some sneaking intuition that, even if all these things needed to be jotted down on the back of an envelope and reread regularly, as soon as we got up speed the wind was going to take it out the window anyway. The Professor's great spiel was about as useful as a love song in a barroom brawl.

But there was one more thing I needed to mention.

"We need a plan B. Contingency. You gotta have a contingency."

"Is that for when we hit the floor?"

"Plan B doesn't take you through the floor. The golden rule is that Plan B has to be just as good as your plan A."

"What is plan A?"

"We do everything we said we would do."

"So what's plan B?"

"Do some of it and then sell."

8

IT CAN'T BE DONE

How to prove the skeptics wrong

"It can't be done," said Tom, throwing up his hands in despair.

"But you said it could be!" I said. "We agreed."

"Yeah, I know," he said. "I was wrong."

"Well, maybe you're wrong now."

We had done the exhibition, we had done the interview, we had announced the existence of the ProDesk 3D to the world. And we had gone over the need for downside protection. The thing we hadn't yet done, admittedly, was produce a real live desktop 3D printer. If we wanted to get it out to punters in "June," we needed to get our skates on.

So we set up for a few days in a house in Nantucket, off Cape Cod. Tom was working on the prototype, trying to get it to fit our vision of what it ought to be. It would be fair to say he had run into a number of technical issues. "I can't get the nozzle to extrude. The cartridges don't all fit. The firmware doesn't work. And the software is nonexistent. It won't print full-color, period."

"But apart from that?"

"Yeah, apart from all that it's fine."

"I have faith, Tom," I said, putting a hand on his shoulder. "A fly-casting world record holder can do anything he sets his mind to."

"I can try, but it's pointless." He gave me a long, weary look. "M, it was a good idea, but we're going nowhere."

"Don't give up, mate," I said, gently. I really did have faith, by the way, I wasn't just saying that to cheer him up. I wouldn't have teamed up with him if I didn't believe. In a way, giving up and shutting down would cost us next to nothing. But in another way we had invested so much in the project already it would wipe us out, the way falling off a big wave and getting pounded does to a surfer. The fact is we both wanted to keep riding it all the way to the beach.

We had both thought we could knock out a ProDesk3D in a matter of weeks. I was beginning to wish I hadn't mentioned "June." It occurred to me I might have to adjust the time frame.

One morning I came down to breakfast. As usual, Tom was fast asleep on the couch. He'd pulled yet another all-nighter. He looked terrible, as usual around this hour: he was wearing a dirty T-shirt and crumpled jeans and his hair was verging on Gorgon. At least he'd taken his shoes off. I made him a cup of black coffee. It was the least I could do.

As I bent down to put the cup on the floor next to him, Tom opened one eye, like Smorg lying on a bed of gold.

"We've cracked it," he groaned, reaching for the coffee.

"You fucking genius, I knew you would." I appreciated his "we," but I thought, credit where credit is due.

"It's not beautiful," he said when he had tidied himself up and brushed his teeth and drunk most of his coffee.

"I can't agree," I said. "It is a thing of rare beauty."

There were bit and pieces all over the places, wires and tubes and clasps, like it was on life support. And it had no lid, so you could see right in. And that was the joy of it, to my way of thinking. I could see the filament snaking across the base. I watched as the nozzle kissed the platform and set about the task of extruding. It had the look of something primal, primitive, like a scene straight out of *Jurassic Park*. The gentle sound of the printer printing was a tinkling brook, like music to my ears.

"What are we printing?" I asked.

"Easiest thing I could think of," Tom said. "A cube."

"That's perfect."

"Just a small one, so it won't take too long." Tom was always modest, but this time there was a note of pride in his voice. "I've specified three colors—yellow, blue, and green."

"My favorite colors," said I.

It was all going so well. We had, I would say, half a cube. About the size of my thumbnail. Multiple colors, exactly as the doctor ordered. And then . . . the machine stopped. Just nothing. No printing, no sound, nada. I looked at Tom. He was looking at the printer with an air of disbelief.

"Is it having a little breather or what?" I asked. "Is that in the script?"

"Er, no, it's not supposed to stop."

I rubbed my eyes as if it had all been a bad dream and when I opened them again everything would be okay. But it wasn't. I spoke with a degree of sadness rather than bitter rebuke. Tom had tried and failed. "I thought for once we were ahead of the game."

"M, we've never been ahead of the game."

We were both broken. For once even I felt like giving up. We were so near and yet so far. It felt like we were just chasing our tails, getting nowhere. I left Tom to it and went out for a walk around the island. I needed to clear my head and forget about 3D printers for a while.

When I returned, several hours later, Tom came rushing out to me. "Look at this," he says, planting something in my hand.

"What is it?" I said.

"It's a vase."

I examined it closely. If it was a vase, it was a vase with numerous twists in, almost like a crumpled ball of paper. From above it looked like a mini–Grand Prix circuit. Or you could say it had waves built into it. It was complex, organic, with no straight edges or flat surfaces—just the kind of thing a 3D printer ought to be good at when it's almost impossible to do it any other way. And it was in several colors with a gentle gradient between them.

"Hold on a second," I said. I went to the kitchen and filled a jug with water. Then I came back into the "lab"—the living room—and poured the contents of the jug into the vase. It was a simple test. "Look!" I cried out. "It holds water!"

"It's a vase, what did you expect?" says Tom, as if it was obvious and nothing could possibly go wrong.

I'm an old hand with a video camera, so the first thing I did was to get Tom to set it all up again. It was "take 2!" Fortunately, the printer printed all over again and we captured the entire process on film, shot from the most favorable angles, and surgically edited— with the final product, a gorgeous and indescribable vase. I poured in the water and plonked in a few flowers. The end. All in sixty seconds flat, after editing. I'd also inserted a few captions at the bottom of the screen.

Presenting, the ProDesk3D
The most advanced 3D printer in the world
The most beautiful 3D printer in the world
Coming soon to a desktop near you

Then I posted it online.

"We've done it," I said to Tom. "You've done it."

"There's still a long way to go," says Tom.

"Yeah, I know, but we've come a long way. Come on, let's go and celebrate."

So we went to the hotel nearby for a drink and something to eat. Maybe at last we really were ahead of the game. Or if not ahead at least we were in it, we were still clinging on to the crest of our wave.

When we got back to the house, I had a quick look to see if there was any reaction to our post. I wasn't really expecting anything. But it turned out there was a ton of comments, all of them negative and skeptical.

"We don't believe!"

"You must have faked it."

"We've been trying to do something like this for years. And I can tell you this: <u>IT CAN'T BE DONE!!!</u>"

Other remarks were not just disbelieving but downright abusive. None of it worried me in the least. We knew it could be done, and we weren't faking it. It might take time, but we would prove the skeptics and the cranks and the haters wrong.

I lit up a cigar and let out a cloud of winner-takes-all-scented smoke.

9

THE THIRD PARTNER

We will therefore never escape manufacturing, even if we are doing the manufacturing in different countries to take advantage of the price benefits. So building a great new product or service with a manufacturer can also be rewarding. (The Professor, Lesson 4)

I have to give a shout-out to a guy who was completely invisible to the general public, but, if you were a customer, possibly more significant than me and Tom. His name was Gary Wiseman. Without him, the ProDesk3D would never have happened. It was our design, but he built it. Ideas are great, but execution is everything.

We had already told everyone that we were "building" our printer. So we thought we had better nail down someone to actually build it—a manufacturer. Without a manufacturer you have nothing but a dream and a pitch. Tom had done the basic engineering, heroically cutting and filing and sawing—and printing!—the parts for the prototype all on his own. He had jerry-rigged the motor and screwed in the tubes. But he had no lathe and no metal-turning skills. So we needed somebody else on the team. It couldn't just be two men in a hot tub any longer.

We scoured China. We contemplated Europe. And then we zeroed in a small industrial estate in the backwoods of New Brunswick, New Jersey, less than an hour out of New York, with—importantly for us—a grand tradition of making. Gary, stocky, bearded, with a fanatical attention to detail that rivaled manic Tom's, was a maker and the son of a maker too.

Of course, you never accept the first quote. We visited four or five potential facilities, but as soon as Tom and I saw Gary's factory, we knew we were in the right place. It wasn't massive, about the size of a modest aircraft hangar, but it was clean and orderly and had everything we needed. There was a test bed and an assembly line and a packaging section, with executive offices upstairs. They had all the right tools and equipment. This was a classic one-stop shop, family run, which could work all the way from raw materials through to delivery.

We both really liked Gary. He was blunt and direct. Gray-haired, fifty-something, stubbly chin, with four decades of experience in the family business. But the key for us was that he was—like us—an enthusiast, a fan. Tom walked him through some of the technicalities, and he became an instant convert to 3D. "I really want this to work," he said more than once. He had the vision and the belief. And, like us, was willing to take risks. We needed someone with not only the machinery but the right mindset too. We saw it in Gary.

In our first face-to-face meeting in his office, I didn't pull any punches. After we had finished talking about how great it was going to be, how fabulously beautiful, how immensely profitable, I took a breath and said, "You realize that this could all go pear-shaped unless we get it dead on."

"Does that mean go to shit?" asked Gary. Every now and then I come out with native English idioms.

"There's a lot that could go wrong."

"Like every other project I've ever got involved in," he said. "I'm not too worried."

"You know it's not going to be easy," I persisted. "We're at the beginning of something. It could be huge—but it could die."

"I can help you prove it works."

That was the dealmaker for me. He had priced in the risk. He was cool and calm and confident, possibly even more confident than he had any right to be. He nodded when Tom showed him his drawing of the new color-extruding nozzle and explained how it needed to work with feeders and a mixer and a central chamber. He was more confident than I was. I was panicking, inwardly. But having given it due thought, he had come to the conclusion that he could make a fortune with the ProDesk3D. We didn't need to make him feel good about the printer, he made us feel good about it. It was like he sold the idea to us. He overcame our doubts about translating the dream into a working machine.

We didn't ask for any discounts (nor did Gary offer). We paid the going rate. For around sixteen months, Gary was going to be investing all his time and energy into our project. He obsessed about the same problems we obsessed about. We couldn't ask for more than that. After that immersion in the hot tub, we had the design or at least the initial concept for a design, but it was Gary who had to make it real. His first task was to build the prototype. For starters he had to source the motors from China. There was a long list of third-party suppliers. We needed to buy in everything, right down to the washers and little things like that. The cost per unit was around $2,250, including all components and labor.

Making the 3D printer was not unlike making a car. With around four hundred moving parts, there were a lot of different elements that had to be integrated if you wanted it to be a goer. That was, in essence, Gary's job: to assemble all the parts. And once you'd stuffed all the different parts of the engine under the hood, it still had to look good. Streamlined. Zero to sixty in a jiffy. Unlike a Porsche, it also had to fit neatly on top of your desk.

I remember saying to Tom, when we walked out of Gary's factory, "If this gets big, we're going to get stuffed." In other words, I wasn't sure we had the resources to cope with a huge surge in demand. After the article and the podcast, we had been inundated with inquiries.

The potential demand was there. But, realistically, at this point in the graph, half a dozen customers would be a spike. If it really took off there were going to be more angry people than printers.

Tom didn't seem too concerned. "We haven't sold any yet. Come to think of it, we haven't made any yet either. So aren't you being a bit presumptuous?"

We were excited, but we were nervous too in just about equal proportions. Tom is a pretty relaxed sort of guy. A bit Zen. Never overly high or low. He'd been in hardware most of his life, so he was used to it. Gary likewise. But I was feeling the stress of trying to get the show on the road. It was like a production of *Hamlet*. You walk out onstage, you've wangled your way into playing the part of the prince, the spotlight goes on, and then you realize, "Oh, shit, I completely forgot to read the play." It was big, it was serious, and we were utterly unprepared.

I can remember one day after another sleepless night where I was brushing my teeth and I looked in the mirror and spat out the toothpaste in horror: I was a freak. My face looked like I had been addicted to crystal meth, gone to rehab, then fallen back into my old habits. I desperately splashed cold water on my face. Even my wife took fright. "You don't look well," she said. "Can you get your 3D printer to print a new husband?"

Gary, in contrast, was like an extension of Tom. They were both calm and focused on the engineering side. Some of the time Tom was virtually living at the factory and sleeping on a couch—if he slept. It was my job to go and sell botObjects. The Professor reminds us that "When building a product, consider using distributors as a fast way to access existing channels and relationships that can span the globe. Giving the distributor a wholesale price and making a decent gross margin on your product can be less expensive, reduce complexity and scale the startup faster." For once I would follow his sage advice. But in the back of my mind was this nagging question of how to get distributors to pay without seeing anything. I was selling something that didn't actually exist. Yet. It was like trying to sell a dream or a prayer.

Naturally cash flow was going to be an issue (for all of us), but we were always on good terms with Gary. I was completely frank with him. In fact I was brutal. I told him everything that was on my mind—except for one big thing. Possibly the biggest thing of all.

I had neglected to tell Gary something he probably didn't want to hear. From day one, I was secretly planning for the exit. We hadn't really got in yet but—getting way ahead of myself—I was already thinking about how to get out. Starting a startup is like being a secret agent: you don't walk in through the front door without making sure there's a back door or a handy window for a nifty escape.

10

THE STORMTROOPER HELMET

Think thin

A great philosopher once posed the tricky question, "Why is there something rather than nothing?" I sometimes wonder about that. But my ever-present fear in 2013 was that our rapidly swelling numbers of customers and distributors—which went from hundreds to thousands almost overnight—would be asking, "Why is there nothing rather than something?"

We had made promises, and now we were under pressure to deliver. I was not aiming to be another Elizabeth Holmes and we were not pulling a Theranos (who, you will recall, offered a world-beating, billion-dollar drop-of-blood analysis system that did not, in fact, exist). "We have solved all the major technical problems," we said, grandly (and theoretically). We had proclaimed the existence of a high-speed high-resolution full-color 3D printer that could sit on your desk and still produce an elephant (perhaps a rather small baby elephant, but still). The fact is we didn't have one. But we had to give them something rather than nothing. Which explains how we came up with the shell or carcass or case—or as Gary called it, thanks to a typo, and the name

47

stuck, the "cake." At least we could say it looked good. Like a wedding cake. Inedible but still. You could say it was a fake cake because there was nothing to eat. But the marriage (in my mind between us and distributors and ultimately customers) would go ahead anyway.

Like a great work of art, it didn't actually "work" or do anything. All it had to do was be. Sit there looking beautiful. It was just a box, in essence, but if we couldn't do function at least we could do form—I hoped. I always thought it looked like an outsize stormtrooper's helmet, uniform and rounded and compact.

We wanted the brushed-aluminum look. Smooth and polished. It would be like an iPhone that you could hold in your hand or put in your pocket but that didn't enable you to call or message anyone. The cake was my solution to the distributor problem: entertain them in New York, take them to the factory, and show them the box. The key thing was not to let them look inside: there was nothing under the hood. It was a car without an engine. But so long as it was sitting in the showroom, it couldn't do any harm, could it? People would get excited just looking through the window.

It's always a million miles from paper to reality. Just because it looks good on the page it isn't necessarily going to work. With the hundreds of moving parts, the dozen motors, and the half a dozen cartridges, the main problem for us—or, more specifically, for Gary—was how we were going to cram it all in. The answer, in the first phase, was by "bulking up." That's what Gary said: "We gotta bulk up."

In other words, the box, like a bodybuilder, was going to have to get bigger to accommodate everything. "You've got all those reels of filament to fit in if you want it to be full color," said Gary. "If you make the case too small you can't get a lot of plastic in there." Black was the predominant color, so that cartridge got double the size.

"It has to look slim," I said. That was my mantra. As slim as a ballerina or a supermodel.

But the first cake that Gary took out of the oven was way too big. More like a quarterback or a Mac truck. Which is exactly what I said (I may have punctuated with a few choice profanities, possibly quite a lot). We knew it had to be reasonably vertical. It needed a base to sit on and a glossy finish on top. "We can stick all the tubes for the filament on the back," I said. "We need to think thin." All the plumbing could be neatly tucked away behind the digital display with information on the print and status of the cartridges.

I sent Tom and Gary back to the factory to do it all again. "I don't want a fucking Saint Bernard," I said. "I want a greyhound." They came back with something like a golden retriever. In theory you should build from the inside out. We built from the outside in and left what it would look like on the inside till later. So we gave it sharper edges to make it look smaller, more angular, more racehorse than workhorse. It would have to do. It resembled a watercooler more than anything, but smooth, almost seamless, one that had just landed from outer space, the creation of a more advanced civilization, which made all its more terrestrial rivals look clunky and primitive, instantly out-of-date.

The best part of it—the cherry on the cake—was the nozzle. Six filaments and six spouts. It looked like a scaled-down version of the flying saucer in *Close Encounters of the Third Kind*. We had already filed the patent, so we sent out a picture of the nozzle by way of stirring up some excitement. "It's coming!"

It was ready to go onstage for the first time. We stuck the word "prototype" on the box, to cover ourselves, to show we knew there would have to be changes.

I was, frankly, as nervous as a debutante. We knew that if we got it right it could be huge. Equally, if we got it wrong it could also be huge—a huge great catastrophe for all of us. A multitude of disappointed customers. Probable bankruptcy, possible court proceedings. That was scary.

I checked back with the Professor: The basic rule on pricing is 45 percent margin, minimum. But of course we needed a "bill of materials." And of course we didn't have one. So there was no way we could calculate what the true costs were going to be. We couldn't give anyone a price until we had come up with the prototype. All we had was a shell with the prototype label stuck on the outside. But we had to give them a price anyway. So we settled on $3k as the baseline. We did a special edition in which the door on the side was colored blue. That was an extra thousand. For a little door. But, to be fair, it was a true collectors' item.

When Gary finally came up with the revised box, I was on Nantucket Island with the family. My wife, who is from Massachusetts, wanted us to find a house there. So Tom brought it to Nantucket together with some other techie who was helping him and then we flew a few people up to have a look at it. In a way it was perfect. We fly you to our remote island—the most easterly part of the United States—to see our top secret project, all expenses paid. And then you can go away and tell everyone about it. We had a distributor from Japan, Hiroshi, and one from England, a journalist called John Biggs (whom I therefore christened Big John), and a photographer called Larry. Big John was quiet and kept his thoughts to himself, but I knew he had already launched businesses of his own and was a true believer in the future of 3D, so I thought he would be on our side. Larry was a cheerful, foulmouthed sort of guy, always obsessing about the light and his camera settings and effing and cussing almost anything good or bad. He made me seem quite polite.

We tried to keep them all entertained while we were getting everything set up. We took them to play football on the beach (in separate shifts—we wanted to keep the distributors away from the journalists in case they got any bad vibes; and it had to be touch football—we thought a broken neck could be a hindrance to sales), we drove them around the island (in different cars), we wined and dined them. Anything to put them in the right mood.

Tom and his crew had the wedding cake all neatly set up in the cottage that was an annex to our hotel. Now all we needed was the guests to come and enjoy it. At last we had something to show them. We put them all in a room with a lovely view over the ocean—decorated with flowers and not a few bottles of champagne. We gave them the big buildup. All the spiel about how revolutionary this machine was in the great 3D printer industry.

Then we opened the doors to our dedicated ProDesk3D room and let them in. They were, in effect, what the Professor likes to call a customer focus group: "This is an exciting stage as you can hear directly what their sentiment is like toward your product or service— try doing this in person, as in case they don't really communicate what they feel, you'll be able to see it in their body language."

We were done with talking the talk. Now we had to walk the walk. We would live or die by what happened next.

11

THE BIG REVEAL

"This wouldn't be the first time 3D printing
has seen a bad actor."

"I really want this thing to be true and real. It would be wonderful. And I will be the first to admit I was wrong and apologize profusely if this incredible idea is real. If this were a concept I would go easy on it but they say they have this device and it will be on the market in weeks. I am highly skeptical. Technically I don't think it's possible, they also don't seem to have the required knowledge of people who would have done this."

Thus said one Joris Peels in a May 2013 post on his blog *VoxelFab* titled "My doubts about BotObjects." We weren't completely cut off in Nantucket. News was still filtering through to us, and, I had to assume to our guests. And it was all negative, or if not negative, then— like Joris Peels's point-by-point deconstruction of one of our press releases—outright skeptical. I couldn't help but notice that, in addition to his skills as a blogger, Peels had been a manager at Shapeways, one of our rivals, and was now a cofounder of Origo, who were also making 3D printers. It was no coincidence that most of the flak was coming straight out of the enemy camp. It was part jealousy, part Machiavellian malice. Blogs were new then, and people sat up and took notice.

Mr. Peels was not alone. The 3D herd was in full cry. *Wired*'s Joseph Flaherty tweeted, "Lack of a proof of concept printed part is especially damning." An anonymous SlashDot poster joined in the chorus of abuse: "So we have computer-generated images of the printer. No images of prints. No images of the device proper. No cost. No details on the 'cartridge system.' No details on the internal mechanics. Claiming capabilities and qualities far beyond what the most advanced/expensive devices on the market can claim." CNET even demanded to know about the engineers involved, where they came from, and whether they were affiliated with a university.

A guy called Rich Brown from CNET interviewed me over the phone, and I was as straight as a die, I swear. I agreed with him that we weren't the first in the field, but we had simply come up with a better mousetrap. And yet he had the almighty cheek to write this: "So far we have only the assurances of botObjects founders that the ProDesk3D is a real product. Their entrepreneurial track record—a business networking site, a film company, a recruiting service—doesn't indicate a history of hardware product development or technology product marketing or manufacturing, but searching their prior dealings also doesn't turn up any malfeasance."[2]

Oh well, at least I wasn't an out-and-out felon—not so far as he could work out. He must have been phoning all his police and prison contacts. So far he'd drawn a blank. But it was clear he was hoping he would discover I had recently been released after serving several years in Sing Sing on charges of fraud and deception. "If botObjects is a scam, this wouldn't be the first time 3D printing has seen a bad actor." Were we bad actors? At least he allowed that "the ability

---

2 Brown, Rich. "BotObjects 3D Printer Promises Huge Leap Forward, Draws Skeptics." CNET, May 10, 2013. cnet.com/tech/computing/botobjects-3d -printer-promises-huge-leap-forward-draws-skeptics/.

to print objects in a full range of colors from common PLA plastic would instantly put the ProDesk3D at the top of the consumer-grade printer market." And he ended on a relatively positive, almost celebratory note:

> If the ProDesk3D is real, it could be a fantastic leap forward for 3D printing. Full-color prints in an attractive, easy-to-use product is the holy grail for this stage of the technology. I would like it to exist, and I'm choosing to remain cautiously hopeful. That position will quickly sour if botObjects starts accepting preorder money without substantiating its claims. We should learn more in a couple of weeks.

We were under surveillance. Our every step was being monitored and scrutinized. Especially when we didn't make one. We were in danger of losing control of the narrative. That was why we had to stage the demo in Nantucket.

The moment of truth had finally come.

"Whoa, looks fuckin' great," Larry exclaimed, loudly. He swooped around the printer, shooting it from all sorts of angles, like a *Penthouse* photographer shooting Pet of the Month. The nozzle was still modestly concealed behind a blanking plate.

Everyone else gathered around at the great unveiling and seemed to be admiring it rather as if it was the latest work of art by Andy Warhol or Damien Hirst. The body language was positive. I saw Tom across the room, and we gave one another a conspiratorial smile like a thumbs-up. It looked as if we were home and dry.

"And over here," I announced grandly, "we have the pièce de résistance." Everyone turned as if they were one—like a school of fish or a flock of birds—to my other showpiece that I had lined up in the opposite corner. "Ladies and gentlemen, I give you: Michelin Man."

Everyone recognizes the Michelin Man and generally feels rather well-disposed toward him, I guess in part because he is as generously endowed as Father Christmas or Falstaff. We had printed one out back at the factory using the prototype machine. Of course Michelin Man is generally white or an off-white color. But that is so old school. We had brought Michelin Man right up to date. Larry was right in there flashing away with his camera. "That is psychedelic, man!" he said.

"I couldn't put it better myself," I said.

We had used all the colors at our disposal. Michelin Man, although a mere six inches high, was like an incarnation of ROYGBIV, with the color gradually shading from one to another. He was now Spectrum Man. The distributors loved it. Michelin Man is the great universal. This is what we were counting on. If we were going to sell the ProDesk3D all over the world then we needed to print something that everybody understood.

It was mission accomplished, as far as I was concerned. We had worked our magic, we had cast the spell over the assembled throng. Now all we had to do was get them out of there as fast as possible, before the effects wore off. Then somebody asked the question I was hoping and praying not to hear.

"Can we see it working now?"

12

"IT'S REAL!"

Seeing is believing

It was that lousy distributor from England. Bastard. I regretted inviting him.

I put on my bravest smile. Fortunately, I had my reply all ready to go, for what it was worth. "Luckily we printed out the Michelin Man earlier. We've had a bit of trouble with the electricity supply since then." This machine was just a box with a few wires in—there was no way it was going to do any printing.

"But the lights are on," said the annoying Brit.

"The energy supply has been fluctuating," I said. But I was flailing around and starting to sound a bit desperate. In the cartoon that was running in my head I was going red in the face and pulling my own hair out. We had a beautiful looking printer—isn't that enough for you? And a beautiful Michelin Man as well? And now you want to see it working too? How unfair is that?

"Fortunately, one has rectified the electrical issue," said the techie guy Tom had brought along. He spoke with a strong French accent. I should have asked who he was but I had been obsessing about machines more than people the whole time. "One added a simple storage device. If you please, allow me to demonstrate." He went to another printer he had already set up in another corner of the room. No one had told me about this. I was panicking but thought it was better to keep my mouth shut for once. The printer wasn't quite as smooth and perfect looking as the one I had prepared to show off to the masses. It was more functional and workmanlike with various tubes and boxes loosely attached to the outside. It wasn't as beautiful as mine, but maybe . . .

He switched it on. Immediately it started to make something on the platform. You could actually see the colors extruding. The audience looked on in amazement—as if they were witnessing a miracle—as the botObject grew in size and complexity. "The firmware is configurable," he said, to fill in the time, "so one can set the base leveling routine and control the fan speed."

The printer head clacked away, disgorging colors like a demented rainbow. A few minutes later and the new creation stood in front of us. It was small but perfect.

"Fuckin' Eiffel Tower!" gasped Larry.

As per Paris, but banded in multiple colors, undreamed of by Monsieur Eiffel, that made it look as if it had been dunked in some mad Neapolitan ice cream. Sometime later that morning I was finally introduced to the man who had in fact saved our bacon. "Meet Gaston," says Tom. He said it with a French accent too.

"You're from France? A cheese-eating surrender monkey?"

"Canada," he said, looking me defiantly in the eye. "Québécois." He looked to be about ten years younger than Tom.

"I love cheese anyway. And ice hockey."

"Our new firmware specialist," said Tom, hurriedly, to stop me mouthing any further cultural stereotypes. He had done exactly what I had asked him to do—to get in "Gaston," who had supplied the open-source firmware that we had been using for our printer. I had no idea he actually was French or French Canadian anyway—I assumed he just nicked the name from *Beauty and the Beast*. But I knew that while I was swanning around in Nantucket, he had got the new rig up and running.

"Glad to have you on the team," I said. "That was a great demo."

"One wanted to pay homage to the country where the internet was born," he said. He spoke excellent English but with a strong accent and a few idiosyncrasies. *Om-marge.* Perhaps his grasp of recent tech history left something to be desired too but one didn't want to quibble (as he might say).

"That's the best thing we've done so far," I said.

"It wasn't too 'ard," he said. "I had a Tour Eiffel on my key ring. All I 'ad to do was scan it . . ."

"Et voilà!" Extracted from my very limited schoolboy stock of French phrases. But a gesture of rapprochement all the same.

Gaston Bachelier turned out to be an essential part of the crew. He tweaked the hell out of the original thousands of lines of code to get the motors accelerating and decelerating in the right places (so as to avoid blobs and oozing) and do the calculations for the slicing software and feed the right colors at the right time from the cartridge to the nozzle. He came from a French-Canadian family, born on the New Jersey side of the Hudson, but raised in Montréal (which he always pronounced "Mon-ray-al"). He was a physicist who had swerved into software. His father made candy bars, and his mother was a sound engineer in a recording studio. He built electronic foosball tables and practiced the double bass when he was not developing new code for the printer or reading books about Chinese medicine. One day when Tom complained of a headache Gaston offered to massage his feet. He said the foot was the main cause of pain in the head. Which made a kind of bizarre sense to me, but Tom thanked him for his kind offer and took some pills instead. Gaston's regulation outfit was jeans and sweater—or a T-shirt if it was warm and a denim jacket when it got cold that made him look like the young Bob Dylan freezing his butt off in New York. But he always managed to look artfully disheveled whatever he was wearing.

Nantucket swung public opinion our way. This was the first article to appear, by Big John, with photographs by Larry, on TechCrunch, which was all about the latest trends. The fairly unspectacular (but, it should be said, reassuring) title was "Hands-on with the botObjects ProDesk3D." But the takeaway was contained in the second line: *it's real!* This is Big John's first paragraph:

> *After months of speculation and quite a bit of skepticism, we're pleased to report that the ProDesk3D is real, it works, and it really does print in color. How, exactly, is still under question—we weren't given direct access to the innards of the machine—but we saw it working with our own eyes.*[3]

You couldn't ask for more from an eyewitness. Perhaps it was on the back of that first vindication that we soon received another accolade. We were on the cover of an issue of *T3* magazine dedicated to the "Hot 100"—the most desirable gadgets—and we were rated number one! We came ahead of smartphones, PlayStation, and Google Glass (and Apple wasn't even in their top ten). I honestly don't know how that happened. Not that I'm complaining. But you'd think we had paid them for that kind of exposure and we didn't, not a cent. *T3* thought, as did almost everyone else at that time, that the 3D printer had the greatest "life-changing potential." And it was the sexiest-looking among a raft of other 3D printers.

Take a bow, Tom and Gary and Gaston. They were the stars of the show: I was just stage manager.

---

3   Biggs, John. "Hands-On with the botObjects ProDesk3D." TechCrunch, September 16, 2013. techcrunch.com/2013/09/16/hands-on-with-the-botobjects -prodesk3d/.

13

@DOUBTINGTHOMAS

Business is war

Was I a fraud? No. Was I an evangelist? Yes, I hope so. Someone had to be.

The fact is, I don't go around putting people down. I always try to be generous in my remarks about the competition. You won't find me saying, "They are so slow!" Or "They're rubbish." But of course you will find me boasting that we have the only printer capable of printing at 25 microns. The only printer with this kind of speed, three times faster than anyone else. And the only printer with full color. The only printer with tri-fan architecture. And when I say it's the "only" one of its kind then clearly, by implication, it is just a little bit of a put-down where everyone else is concerned. At best they were two-color. And had two fans. We were the new kids on the block. And the old guard were feeling the heat. Maybe they could do with some tri-fan architecture?

I'm a promoter. I have this habit of pushing the boat out, when it deserves a good push. When I met Bre Pettis, the cofounder and CEO of MakerBot—which was like an earlier incarnation of botObjects and in many ways our role model—I told him flat out: We can do a better job. Whenever I was interviewed (at its height, at least once a day), I told everyone, from reporters to bloggers to distributors: We can do better. I was only saying what I thought and believed. What was the point in saying anything else? Should I have said how nice their printers were? Maybe that would have been diplomatic, but I honestly thought I was helping them—they needed to get up to speed, they needed to acquire full color too. It was obvious, surely. I was stating the obvious. It really was "a giant leap for 3D printing." Resolution has to be high, and speed has to be fast. The build envelope has to be big. People want what they want. Who wants low quality? Anything you can do we can do better. Obviously. And yet there was something about the way I put it—despite, as I say, not putting anyone down exactly and not setting out to upset anybody—that seemed to wind people up. Somehow I succeeded in pissing off the entire industry. Who does this guy think he is, telling us we're not good enough? Who says we need to innovate? We already innovated! Maybe he needs to be taught a lesson. It was a bit Robert De Niro in *Taxi Driver.* "You talkin' to me?"

It's sad really. But this deep background might help to explain how it was we ended up becoming the object of twenty-nine separate acts of defamation. An immense bunch of sour grapes. All in just one article. By a blogger.

After the big reveal, we made a couple more videos of the machine working. To reassure the world at large that it was fully operational. We had innovated and proved that it worked. We even showed the internals this time, like Amazon's "Look Inside." Let them cry fake, but you'd have to be Steven Spielberg or Industrial Light & Magic to fake it that well. Or so I thought. We lugged the machine around conferences and exhibitions all over the world to convey the simple message: It was real, real, real. Seeing is believing, isn't it?

But all in vain. There were still people out there—possibly the same people who don't believe we ever landed on the moon—who reckoned we had somehow faked the whole thing. Some guy made a video of how to print a colored object using tie-dye to paint the colors on. A "forensic photographer" was brought in by *Wired* magazine to "prove" with "high certainty" that everything we had done was a simulation. The wooden surface we had put the printer on was clearly rendered by computer (it was a standard office desk). The "conflicting shadows" (well, there were two light sources!) demonstrated that we were cutting and pasting. It was too perfect. None of it was real.

One morning, very early, sometime after Nantucket, I was rudely awoken by the phone ringing on Long Island (yes, I actually have an old landline phone next to my bed). It was Tom. He was in a spin. "Have you seen the latest edition of Tech for Breakfast?"

"Tom, it's a bit early."

"It's like a declaration of war."

"Don't sweat it," I said, trying to soothe him. "Business is war. You need enemies. So long as we have a few defenders." It was an old slogan of mine. You are basically Clint Eastwood caught in a cross fire between two camps (as in *A Fistful of Dollars*). But that was okay, there would be a way to profit from both of them. If we didn't have a few enemies, that's when I would start to worry. Think of a chess game—there's a lot of gratuitous violence. You basically want to blast the other guy off the table, to wipe out their army.

"Read it," said Tom, not in the least placated. "You won't like it."

So, eventually, I read it. Tom had a point. The whole article, written under the nom de guerre "@DoubtingThomas," was a massive takedown of botObjects and me in particular. It had "FAKE" in the title. After all our efforts. The word "scam" came up a lot in relation to the ProDesk3D. As did "fraud" with reference to me. Not to mention the word "crook." The box, according to Doubting Thomas, was just a box with absolutely nothing inside it. It was all smoke and mirrors and CGI. Apparently our whole mission was to rip off gullible consumers. We were planning to take the money and run. We really ought to be locked up to prevent us from carrying out our crimes. And so on. They were crucifying me. It was a good story—for readers. But it had put a bomb right under botObjects. This was more than just journalistic skepticism—it was manifest malice. Like letting one of the Borgias loose with a keyboard. If this was a chess game, I was going to lose a knight or two. We needed a strategy.

I was pacing up and down, reading it on the phone at home. "Can you stop pacing?" my wife said.

"I'm taking fucking bullets here!" I said, slapping myself on the chest.

"And can you stop swearing? Here, have a sweet." She has a stash of those long-lasting mints around for when I need calming down. It shuts me up for a while. I sucked one, but the article still left a nasty taste.

You need antagonists, but every now and then you have to make them pay. I took the article into Patrick's office and got him to read it while I sat there. Patrick was our silver-maned company lawyer. He had been a barrister back in the day, but we had persuaded him to come and work for us exclusively. He was around 250 pounds and hadn't seen the inside of a gym for a while and he had this odd habit of falling asleep at his desk and then toppling off his chair onto the floor but then remaining fast asleep. Sometimes we would be working downstairs and we would hear this great thud above us on the ceiling and we would look at one another and say, "Patrick's nodded off again."

But he was wide awake on this particular day. This article was like meat and drink to him. The worse it was the better he liked it. He looked up at me, grinning, and said one word, "Sue!"

He reckoned there were dozens of defamatory statements and flat-out falsehoods. I wasn't sure I needed the distraction, but he didn't think they should be allowed to get away with it.

So we sued.

And we won.

Or were going to. Tech for Breakfast wisely settled out of court. In the end they accepted that the author had committed a grand total of no less than twenty-nine separate libels against me and bot-Objects. They had to eat humble pie and withdraw everything and expunge the article from existence. Patrick had been right. He was our defender, no matter if he did fall off his chair from time to time.

The scam story was just plain wrong, inspired by nothing but jealousy. It turned out that Doubting Thomas—or Tamsin—had been sponsored by one of our embittered competitors. Our printer was never a scam: maybe "ambitious," possibly "overambitious." Or how about "ahead of its time"?

Is all publicity good publicity? The Professor says, "Be the storyteller." Sound advice, but as soon as your back is turned people are going to be telling stories about you. To my way of thinking, there is the good, the bad, and the downright ugly. We had all three. But when Riley Griffin at Mimetics3D (much bigger than us and way more established) dropped by, he said, "We're not getting the press you're getting. You're getting better PR than any of us. What's your secret?"

The Professor didn't say, "There's only one thing in life worse than people talking about you—people not talking about you," but maybe he should have.

14

ROFI THE ROBOT

Never say no

One day, out of the blue, in the summer of that year of wonders, Fox Business News contacted us. First it was an underling in their press office who had been reading up on our exploits, and then the esteemed Stuart Varney, Fox Business presenter. Could they do a live interview? And could we bring along something we had printed out?

Never say no is my default position. I mean, look at the very long list of "Marketing Channels (Large and Small)" in "Marketing for Effective Customer Acquisition" (Entrepreneur Seminar, Lesson 3): "Film/TV Product Placement" is right up there, between "Facebook page" and "Forums." Even so, Tom wasn't too keen. He thought we weren't ready. It wasn't ready. But, as I explained to him, it was all part of the job, it was what we signed up for. We're either all in or we're out. No chickens.

"Okay, then," he says. "It has to be a robot."

I thought about it for about a tenth of a second. "Perfect," I said. "That's botObjects in one." Maybe, in hindsight, we were getting ahead of ourselves.

Turns out that Tom didn't even plan to build a 3D printer in the beginning. What he really wanted to build was a robot. He had shut up shop and taken two weeks off at Christmas, and Tom being Tom he couldn't just sit around and open presents and eat too much pudding. No, he had to have a project, otherwise he got bored. Maybe he was lonely or something, because he decided he needed to build himself a robot friend. It would have to walk on its own, maybe talk too. How hard could it be? He came across a project on a university website with open-source software. He went out and bought all the nuts and bolts and motherboard. Then he ran into a small stumbling block: To build it, you really needed a 3D printer.

Fuck! It was the middle of the Christmas holidays. And he couldn't exactly go out and buy a 3D printer—they were hellishly expensive and not great quality anyway. Tom assumed he could do better. So he went back to his search engine and looked up "How to build your very own 3D printer." If he wanted to build a robot he had to build the 3D printer first. Welcome to Tom O'Brien's life. Many false starts and stumbles and failures and refinements and nozzles and a lot of sleepless nights later, we come to the original pink whistle. But now, finally, Tom was determined to build the robot of his dreams, using the botObjects printer to fabricate the whole thing. Fox Business News had given him just the excuse he needed.

We turned up at the television studio in New York with all our kit and set it up on the desk in front of us. Our kit, on this day, consisted of "Rofi the Robot" (so named by Tom's three-year-old son). To be honest, there had been a few teething problems with Rofi. All of his main body parts came out of the ProDesk3D. Then we put them together and added only the motor and some software. Rofi looked like a real robot—in red and yellow, colors so flashy that people thought we must have painted them on. With multicolor feet, just because ("Impossible!" roared the skeptics). It was a big step up from Michelin Man. Rofi could move, he could go forward and backward, right and left. His legs were operational. There was only one small problem with Rofi—he (I hope "he" won't mind if I call him he) had a habit of tottering and toppling. When he walked he walked with a distinct limp. And then, as a rule, he fell over. He found it hard to maintain the perpendicular.

"Tom, you've got to fix Rofi!" I raged. "He's going on TV. At the moment he's going to embarrass us in front of the whole fucking world." He was Tom's baby. Tom was the robot doctor.

"There's nothing really wrong with him," said Tom, unflappable as ever. "It works."

"But he can't fucking stand up straight!" I pointed out.

"Maybe I shouldn't have used that open-source software. It's something to do with the rechargeable battery. Don't worry, he'll be right on the night." His word for Rofi was "unstable." A bit of a euphemism, I thought, for a robot that couldn't walk in a straight line. If he fell over, we fell right along with him, right into business hell. We would be laughingstocks around the 3D world.

He told me, repeatedly, not to worry. But I did worry. Because an inability to stay upright for much longer than three steps would not look good on a live show. Those skinny little legs just weren't strong enough. Maybe he could be Rofi the Drunken Robot? Come the night, or rather morning, of the show, Rofi was still unpredictable, precarious, as wobbly as a house of cards in a high wind. We had to control the risks. "He'll be fine," says Tom, despite all the evidence to the contrary. "Don't let him out of your hands," I whispered, as we went into the studio. "Please." And I don't often say please.

Inwardly we were panicking, big-time. I like to imagine we looked reasonably calm and composed. Stuart Varney, a suave older white guy, was perfectly amiable. He admired Rofi, who had been featured on the screen several times before our segment. He nicely introduced him as a "3D printed robot." Rofi scored. And Varney gave botObjects a good shout-out. Then he hit us with his bombshell. "I dare you to make that thing walk toward me." Had he heard a rumor?

I could see Tom was tempted. He had more faith in Rofi than I did. He didn't think "unstable" was necessarily the end of the world. I thought he was going to let him loose for a moment. With the emphasis on loose. I nearly fell off my chair. Then he says, "Look, how nicely his legs move." But he didn't make the mistake of putting his feet on the ground: they were dangling in the air. "Rofi's what we call a bipedal robot," In truth he looked more like Pinocchio swinging his legs around with Tom as puppet master.

I rushed to divert attention from Rofi with talk about how revolutionary our printer was. How differentiated. (Here I was only following *The Entrepreneur's Book of Secrets*: "In differentiation, not in uniformity, lies the path of progress," secret #14). How it was twelve times faster (okay, slight exaggeration). An Apple among printers. I made sure to slip in the name ProDesk3D a couple of times at least—a little bit of brand recognition. The pressure was, I thought, off. Varney seemed to agree with us that anyone with our printer could make anything, up to and including a "flying saucer." He called me a "young man" and said I had a nice British accent, but rather spoilt the effect when he added that "People will believe anything you say with a British accent."

Then Varney's bad cop cohost, Charles Payne, younger and a bit more aggressive, mentioned something about Hewlett-Packard coming into the market. As if we were doomed to fail. And how there were printers for $300 (there aren't). He doubted our machine would get beyond the "hobbyist market" at best.

And then Varney starts in about how expensive it is and how he wouldn't buy one. Finally, he reverts to his original theme: "I really want you to put that thing [Rofi] down and let him walk over to me."

We had a good laugh about that.

But we didn't let him "walk" anywhere. Maybe one day, but he wasn't ready yet.

Not our finest hour, but at least it wasn't a total disaster either. Our big mistake was letting a robot be the story. We could have ended up falling flat on our faces along with Rofi.

You can call it a draw. We got our message out. And a picture of the ProDesk3D flashed up on the screen for a brief while. Good advertising. But I thought, "Okay, next time, we are going to give you a live demo of the printer printing in real time." At least it wouldn't fall over and flop—I hoped.

15

THE INTERVIEW

Don't forget the software!

He was not, on the face of it, the most immediately impressive candidate. On the other hand, he stood out for his sheer taciturnity. It was like trying to interview Clint Eastwood, or possibly Clint Eastwood's mule.

"Dylan" (his adopted name) Obeyesekere looked good on paper and had a rare skill set that our expensive specialist recruitment website had put up in neon lights. He had done what most software developers had done. He had played a lot of video games as a kid, and started making up games of his own. Achieved a decent level of technical proficiency at school and college and gone on to work with more than one company in programming. Now in his mid-twenties, he was a top man when it came to coding, but his communication skills were not his strongest suit.

He mumbled a hello when he walked in. No, not hello, more hi. Well, a syllable or a stray phoneme. I want to make clear, in a spirit of diversity, that the ring through the nose didn't worry me at all. I only note that it was there. I couldn't help thinking, though, that that particular piercing must surely be rather painful. (I believe that there is one more area in which piercing could be even more painful, but I was not about to inquire further.) I might add, he had several more rings through his ears too. And one earlobe stretched longer than the other. I wouldn't fancy it, but each to his own.

He was wearing a short-sleeved T-shirt bearing the slogan, "MOSTLY HARMLESS." I recognized the allusion to *The Hitchhiker's Guide to the Galaxy* (in which it is planet Earth that is described that way). The thing that surprised me was that it was a particularly chilly day and he must have been freezing, but that clearly did not concern him. Maybe that is a good sign in a software guy.

And he was wearing open sandals. In the middle of winter. Also promising.

I should stress: We were not in a hurry to hire busloads of fresh young recruits. Bear in mind what our old friend the Professor has to say: "For example, hiring four people for $50K per year with $100k in the bank, means that you'll run out of funds within 6 months—naturally, even with the most aggressive belief in your product or service, this is likely to run into a 'no cash you crash' scenario." But every now and then you are going to have to plug the gaps, and there were a lot of gaps, believe me (or, as the Prof puts it more elegantly, "The other side is recognizing what functions are essential, and what skills you will require").

Tom and I had a problem. I actually woke up sweating about it one night and couldn't get back to sleep. We had finally defined how everything should work and, in particular, what the nozzle should be doing. The extrusion worked just fine. We could accelerate and decelerate going around corners to prevent the ugly blob problem. The temperature at which the object was cooked was, as Goldilocks would say, just right. We had perfected the system of fuse dumping and purging. Gaston had finessed the firmware, so the machine had a brain and it would give appropriate instructions to the nozzle. It knew what it had to do. The camera would scan, and an STL file primed for FFF would describe the geometry of the 3D object, and slice it up into convenient layers for the printer to print. It could virtually teleport you (at least it could if you were made of plastic). But but but . . . had we undercooked the software? Had we, in fact, forgotten all about it? Or at least how complicated it might be?

We had tweaked and finessed and calibrated and primed. Hallelujah!—it worked. But what happened when the average consumer got ahold of one of our printers? Power on. Green light. And then? Of course our hypothetical customer would like to get it fully operational, to ask the ProDesk3D to print, shall we say, a new protective case for their iPhone, or a reusable flask for the gym. The user had to be able to give instructions to the printer and tell it, for example, what color(s) they wanted. Which is where the software comes in. Should it be a pink whistle or a yellow whistle or, then again, a multicolor whistle? Therein lay the rub. We had to be able to get the end user talking to the machine itself. They had to be able to communicate. But you couldn't assume they were talking the same language. Our machine was fluent in a variation on C++; the user might have a basic command of English or Spanish or Japanese. How were they going to speak to one another? How are you going to tell the printer which color filament to pump in? You had to get from the computer screen all the way through to the physical object. Without that it was useless.

Which explains how we came to ask our interviewee, Dylan, with the nose ring, did he think he could solve this problem and get the customer and the machine to understand one another? He was sitting in a chair across the room from us in our New York office. We tried to keep it as informal and unintimidating as reasonably possible. We were sitting in chairs too—we weren't behind a desk. It was nothing like the Spanish Inquisition.

Dylan didn't seem in the least flustered by the question. Most people fished around and floundered. He didn't. He had a simple answer. "Yeah," he said. Not yes but yeah. We waited in vain for anything further by way of clarification. I assumed he had done something similar in his previous posts.

"Oh well," says I, filling the void. "That's reassuring. Good to know, don't you think, Tom?"

"Yes," says Tom. "Definitely." He had his hands folded and was tapping his thumbs together, as if that was going to help much.

"So what do you think you would do exactly," I said, "in a little more detail, to achieve this goal—enabling the end user to send instructions to the printer?"

Dylan had been looking wistfully out of the window. Now he turned his gaze to me for a moment. "I'll think of something," he said, in a tone somewhere between boredom and indifference.

The Professor has a long list of "Key Questions to Draw out Insight from the Candidate." But he was assuming the candidate would have something to say for himself. I tried one of them anyway. "What is your biggest weakness?"

He gave the question careful thought. "M&M's," he replied, finally.

"He's 'mostly harmless,'" I said to Tom when Dylan had left the room.

"He's not the most inspiring," he said.

"Is he the One? Is he our Neo?"

"It's hard to know."

Sometimes, I thought, Tom could be as unforthcoming as Dylan. A bit more articulate, to be fair, but he was never going to be hosting *Saturday Night Live*. And, it occurred to me, if Tom is like Dylan, then perhaps Dylan could be like Tom. Tom had cracked all the problems on the hardware side, maybe Dylan could do the same when it came to software. He only had a matter of weeks to get the job done. We couldn't keep on interviewing people.

"I think we should give him a try." If the one-liners could work for Clint Eastwood, maybe they could work for Dylan.

"Agreed," says Tom.

"What's the worst that can happen?"

16

THE DEMO

"Don't wait for perfection." (The Professor)

The problem was that everything had to be done yesterday, or at the latest today. I think we gave him, in reality, a couple of weeks. His mission was to come up with a piece of software that we could easily post on our website and that could be downloaded by the user when they received the printer, and then installed on their phone or computer. The basic vision was to have Emily (to introduce a random name) unpack her printer, download Dylan's software to her phone, and then immediately print a vase or, let us say, a garden gnome. Lots of colors. All easy to control. That, as I say, was the vision. But could it be achieved in practice?

Dylan promised that it would be. This was the moment of truth.

Come the day of the demo, we were all lined up in the War Room, Tom, Gary, Gaston, Eden (sales), and Jack (customer service). And me. Dylan was standing by the printer.

"You have to imagine I'm the user," he says.

"No, that won't do," says I. "You can't have a developer testing his own code. You know too much. Let me be the user. I know virtually nothing."

"No problem," he said. Unfazed as usual. Not too bothered either way.

"I'm sending you a link."

I clicked on the link and downloaded the app to my phone.

I chose to print a simple eggcup. Small so it would be quick. Then there was the question of color. "How about cyan?"

"No problem," said Dylan, who had a limited number of set phrases for all situations. "No problem" was one of his favorites. Cyan is a standard inkjet color. But it's the kind of color that people will have arguments over—is it blue? Is it green? Answer, it's both. We produce it by overlaying blue on green. It's the color of the Mediterranean around certain Greek islands or the sea in Tahiti maybe. It's the color of lapis lazuli. And now it was going to be the color of my eggcup. So Dylan says, "You should be able to tap in cyan on your app."

I tapped it in. It came up. No problem, as Dylan would say.

The printer started its job of spraying layer on layer on to the platform. The nozzle whizzed around like a whirling dervish.

Tom and Dylan and I stood watching.

It didn't take too long.

The printer sighed and died. Its job was done.

At the end of a few minutes my eggcup stood before us. Totally black. Or possibly charcoal. What it wasn't was cyan. I instantly started to regret my decision to recruit Dylan. I had interpreted his inability to communicate as a sign of genius; clearly it was more likely to be a sign of incompetence—or madness? I couldn't help but think how easy the Professor made recruitment sound: Avoiding the pitfalls of recruitment, once you know them, you can avoid them. Where had we gone wrong?

PITFALLS IN RECRUITMENT (In no particular order:)
1) Underestimating the hiring process
2) Failing to look holistically at the recruiting options
3) Lack of specificity in the candidate spec & résumé
4) Not assessing the level of experience correctly

5) While being prescriptive, having an open mind to candidate experience

6) Not evaluating all the candidate information to hand

7) Not selling and packaging the role correctly

8) Set a target hire time frame and don't wait for perfection

Now I come to think about it, we had probably committed all the above sins. As usual, we rushed it: we were desperate. At least we hadn't "waited for perfection." But clearly we hadn't done our "due diligence" (as per Secret #55 of *The Entrepreneur's Book of Secrets*). We had hired the village idiot.

"What the fuck?" I exploded, concisely summarizing all the above professorial considerations. The rest of the crew looked at their shoes.

I think I could have predicted what Dylan would say. "No problem."

He pulled out his phone and tapped in a few lines of code, then pressed send.

The printer gave a little squeak to acknowledge receipt.

"Try it now." At least it was three words rather than two.

We started all over again. I clicked on cyan.

I didn't think I'd give him three shots—it was two strikes and you're out. We needed someone else.

The printer stopped chattering.

My second eggcup emerged from the machine.

Cyan.

It was like my humble little eggcup had been dipped in the most brilliant ultramarine sea.

Cue applause all round.

Maybe we really could get customers and printers talking to one another. Even if the chance of Dylan and yours truly saying much to one another was extremely limited.

17

THE LAUNCH

*The Professor says, "I often refer to entrepreneurship as a
roller coaster of up and down emotions."*

Eden Burberry pushed us out on the stormy sea. Which was appropriate given that she was a surfer with white hair (not blonde, white,
the effect, she said, of salt and terror). She was also an ex-academic and
ex-journalist and marketing supremo who had embraced the short
form of Twitter. As our newly recruited head of communications, she
was our resident tweeter. And she had a great name, half-paradise,
half-raincoat, ready for anything.

We had done the demo. We had survived the pushback. It only
remained to launch. Tom wasn't confident we had yet solved all the
problems. "So we're taking orders for something we haven't built yet?"
He hadn't fully grasped some of the finer points of entrepreneurship.

"Tom," says I, "this industry is moving so fast. If we don't get ahead
of it, we are going to get left behind. This is the first draft. Nothing is
ever perfect the first time around. Look at the iPhone. Why do you
think they have an iPhone 2 and 3 and 4? We can do that."

"I'm worried people won't be satisfied."

I knew exactly how he felt. I was probably at least as anxious as he was. There were a thousand problems to solve every day. But that was situation normal. "We have no choice," I said. "You can't get anywhere without putting it all on the line." It was risk versus reward. "We have to be tigers." That was a Professor-type thing to come out with. It's probably somewhere in *The Entrepreneur's Book of Secrets*, secret #99. But the fact is that I wasn't feeling anything like a tiger. Not exactly a mouse. Maybe more like an antelope, poised for flight. But I didn't want Tom to know that.

He grumbled, but basically agreed. He was a perfectionist at heart. But total perfection could take a very long time. And we might not be alive to see it either. The Professor, of course, could tell us everything we ought to have done:

PRODUCT PRELAUNCH REVIEW CHECKLIST
1. Market assessment adoption confirmation
2. Sales material generation
3. Product testing go-ahead
4. Sales execution plan formulated, pitch acceleration and training conducted
5. Support documentation authored
6. Customer support function created
7. Customer user interface fully tested
8. Product metrics designed and ready to capture
9. Product pricing confirmation
10. Product marketing and PR plan completed
11. Product/order fulfillment planned and ready to scale
12. Completed your user feedback integration throughout your product experience
13. Created product goals for the product launch & beyond
14. Confirmation of product fully integrated into organization and executive roles, including launch timings
15. Legal agreements in place
16. Road map for product continuity

Could we check a single one of these seemingly simple and yet impossible boxes?

Postscript: Don't avoid any of them—you'll find traps in all of them if they're not well thought through.

Great, thanks, Mr. Know-It-All.

In the end we compromised on a "soft launch"—online only. We couldn't exactly plonk our printers on the display shelves in JCPenney, amid the Apples and the Samsungs and Hewlett-Packards—not yet.

We went live with our preorder book in July 2013. Eden tweeted out a picture of the ProDesk3D. "It's coming!" she wrote, with exemplary concision. (And, in case you're wondering, yes, it is a line I've used before—well, it was coming, wasn't it? It just hadn't come yet.) Her subsequent countdown put me in mind of the countdown in David Bowie's *Space Oddity*. Personally I had little experience of Twitter at the time, and I felt exactly like Major Tom to Ground Control—we were stepping through the door in a most peculiar way. And we might disappear into space or burn up in the atmosphere. Can you hear me Major Tom?

I was certain you couldn't make any money on social media. The crusty old Professor was not a fan. The fact is there are so many things we don't know. That I don't know. But Eden knew what she was doing. She wrote a regularly updated blog on the latest developments and embedded it on Twitter.

At this point we still weren't fully convinced that we would find many or any takers. Maybe all the naysayers had had an impact. But as soon as Eden pressed the button, we were getting thousands of inquiries. People liked the photo. Overnight our followers shot up by thousands. We received over one hundred preorders in just a few days. And they were all paying up front, to the tune of around $400,000. They were queuing up, and it was like there was a line around the block. Our little ProDesk3D was the next big thing. It was like we'd invented cold fusion. Without even trying, we had created a feeding frenzy. We had, almost accidentally, become the leaders in the field, even though we didn't have a printer we could deliver.

Our early adopters, mainly geeks and industry insiders, were almost like a cult. I remember that someone said it was "like Waco all over again." But the fact is they were patient. They had faith. I took a call from one guy in Perth, Australia. An ordinary customer. By some fluke it came straight through to me. I remember his name, because it was a weird one: Rudyard. Rudyard was amazed to be speaking to the CEO. He thought we had the best customer service.

"It's beautiful," he said. "The ProDesk3D. You could put it in a museum."

"We are making as many as possible," I said. "As soon as possible. We are cranking up production as we speak."

"It's a real work of art." He ordered Blue. The more expensive one with the blue door. Rudyard was my favorite kind of customer. I think that was the moment I knew people were really interested in our product. The funny thing was—we hadn't even finally settled on the exact size of the printer: Tom was still working on it.

So we were both elated and panic-stricken by the initial success. How could we possibly deliver?

But Eden was doing nearly all the hard work of communication. She kept the customers in a state of perpetual suspense. They were all waiting with bated breath to see what botObjects would come up with. But, as I say, they were willing to wait.

Not so the distributors. I love distributors, don't get me wrong. But sometimes they remind me of crocodiles, circling—friendly crocodiles. But still. This is a fact—they came to us, such was the power of industry gossip. From far and wide. After a certain amount of haggling, we ended up with distributors from twenty-one countries, from Germany to Japan, from the UK to New Zealand: Australia, Russia, Spain, Mexico. Each one had to pay up to half a million up front, especially China, but I gave a discount to Holland (I had to beg them not to let anyone else know). Half a million was the maximum: it was basically a goodwill gesture, because otherwise I would have to do due diligence. And I didn't have time for due diligence. We raised $15.5 million in venture capital—but we didn't need it. We had proof of market—there was genuinely global demand.

Distributors begged me, very nicely, to get involved. But then, after a short while, they start eating you. We had a constant battle on our hands from media, consumers, but above all distributors. They were sensitive to any straw in the wind. Some of our old allies turned against us. Even SolidSmack, hardened geeks though they were, went over to the dark side. I remember being particularly annoyed by one article when they didn't even spell my name right. That was the worst. I had the feeling they wanted to see us fail. And of course, every time they mentioned the word "scam," it spooked the distributors. Which was not entirely fair, because all it came down to was a small difference of approach toward chronology: they—distributors, customers, and media types—were Newtonian sticklers for the great universal clock according to which we were falling well behind schedule, whereas we were more progressive, Einsteinian, and relativistic in overall conception and felt that since we were speeding up, then time should really slow down to let us finish the job.

One of the heroes fighting the good fight was Jack, our customer support expert. I suppose Eden was our first line of defense, but the backstop was Jack. His job was, essentially, to fend off inquiries. He would spend all day talking to distributors and customers, calming them down and giving them the good news (always assuming there was any). It was probably just as well he was built like a long-distance runner—he was going to need the stamina. His only problem is that he was a sensitive, thin-skinned sort of guy and he took it to heart when people would say, "I'm going to come and hunt you down, you bastards!"

I remember one meeting in the War Room—at the long table in our "campus" HQ—where Jack reckoned he had finally run out of excuses. He was like Zazu in *The Lion King*—he told us what people were saying, even if we didn't necessarily want to hear it. "Jack," I said. "Look at it this way, they're in good company. If Apple can delay their product, anyone can. Same with Tesla—if you want to be an early adopter, you have to face delays. It comes with the territory. They're buying a piece of tech history—the first true full-color desktop 3D printer."

Jack took a lot of the flak. It wasn't a particularly comfortable ride for him. He didn't have the risk—we had the risk—but he did a great job of hiding the risk. I never felt that nervous about the clamor, because it was a lot better than total silence. And the underlying truth was that we—Tom and I—were as honest as the day was long. We didn't suddenly wake up one day and say we know it all. We were just two guys who took the 3D printer industry by storm. We never conned anybody. We might have allowed them to be a little more optimistic than was strictly justified. But we never wavered in our belief that we were the good guys. We didn't chase the money—this wasn't a get-rich-quick-scheme—we really wanted to change the industry for the better. "I often refer to entrepreneurship as a roller coaster of up and down emotions," as the Prof neatly puts it. "We need to ignite the spirit by tapping into our passion. The bottom line is you cannot be mildly interested in your pursuit." We had the passion in spades. We had the belief. We were not faking it.

And yet. The crocodiles had a point, to be fair: We had taken their money, we had promised two or three months' delivery—and hitherto we had delivered nothing. For some reason the distributors in Japan were particularly unhappy. I was in London at the time. Hiroshi flew over to see me and I took him for lunch to George, the Mount Street club. I plied him with food and drink and gave him a cigar to smoke, but still at a certain point he had to ask, "When are we going to get our first printer? Next week maybe?"

"Come on," I replied, "even Google couldn't do it that fast!"

I think Jung would have called it synchronicity. But it was like rubbing a magic lamp. For, behold, at that very moment, Eric Schmidt walked past the window (i.e., the CEO of Alphabet; i.e., Google). And he came in and sat down to lunch with a woman friend. My Japanese distributor friend was completely gobsmacked, as if I had magic powers and could readily beam up anybody from anywhere. The serendipitous manifestation of Eric Schmidt in our midst gave my story a perverse kind of credibility. If I could conjure up the head of Google, then finally coming up with the promised 3D printer should be a piece of cake.

18

THROUGH A GLASS DARKLY

You have to have business faith

At this point in the narrative, you may well be wondering: Why didn't we just give up, Tom and I, call it a day, and give everyone their money back? Couldn't we just walk away and save our sanity? And we definitely thought about it. But there was something that stopped us doing that.

I remember, about twenty years ago, saying, begging, protesting, praying, "Please, God, don't let X die!" As a matter of fact, X lived. But, ungratefully enough, I soon retracted my spontaneous plea to the Almighty: It seemed to me that there were a thousand and one different reasons why X would either live or die, but God wasn't one of them. I used to read the Bible obsessively as a kid, so I'm a reluctant atheist. I think God is a fine idea but lacks any discernible objective correlative. I would agree with Bertrand Russell that if I were to die and go to heaven I would say to God, "Why did you not provide more tangible evidence for your existence?" Once I was asked to say grace at a Thanksgiving dinner. There was a murmur of surprise when I suggested we might want to give thanks to the Big Bang and

84

the universe and the Milky Way and an awful lot of random quantum collisions for our existence. To my way of thinking, intelligent design only began sometime around the first adze or sharpened stone. Nevertheless, I do have faith.

I have business faith. You can't survive long without it. Aristotle says it is natural to seek knowledge. And so it is. But if you're seeking it that means you don't have it, yet. They say we work in a knowledge economy, but that is just tech propaganda. What we don't know far outstrips what we do know. For example, I have no idea if anyone is going to read this book (I can only hope). The fact is that at best we (and here I find myself in agreement with 1 Corinthians, 13:12) see through a glass darkly. When you start up a company, you know that you do not know. You are ignorant about the future. I'm a factologist, and one very sobering fact I do know is that over 70 percent of all new companies will become extinct after five years. You must pray yours will not be one of them. Across this yawning chasm of unknowing, you have to make the leap of faith, in the direction of the confident expectation that your business will flourish and grow.

Which is why I had to become an evangelist. I needed to install the sense of a mission in the whole botObjects crew. I suppose in a way we were like a cult and I was indoctrinating them. I was the Maharishi of printer tech, guiding my followers toward 3D enlightenment. As per my own personal guru, the Professor, "Over-communicate goals, actions, practices so that there is minimal danger of misunderstanding, and more opportunity to correct." But the best way to get the message across was to be the message, to embody belief.

I don't have the apocalyptic mindset. I think, one way or another, beset by uncertainties and black swan events as we are, the world will keep on turning (this side of the sun blowing up into a red giant). I was once given the responsibility of preventing the Y2K millennial meltdown in the institution I was working for at the time. Easiest job I ever did. Nothing happened. I can't claim any credit for that either. It's just we have a habit of anticipating doom. I don't. With a few inevitable deviations and downswings—the "corrections"—I expect the graph to keep going up and to the right.

It's like a chess game. I always assume I will win, even though I don't, not always (especially now my sons are getting better at the game than I am). But what I do know is that if I start off thinking I will lose then I certainly will lose. I don't factor in defeat. What I do is play multiple games, then I know I'll win, at least some of the time.

After SolidSmack turned against us, and we went from "Awesome, dude!" to "Scam!" or "Hoax!" my faith was momentarily shaken, I have to admit. They were our stout pillar—and then they weren't. We had been relying on them to see us through. It was like, "Please, SolidSmack, don't let botObjects die!" (Another version would be "Stop killing us, you bastards!") But then I recovered and I realized that there were a thousand and one factors that could lead to us living or dying. There were many other times when I was on the verge of losing faith—for example, every time we missed another deadline; and every time the printer gave up the ghost and we had to resuscitate.

When I was around fifteen and I was winning a lot of chess games and, of course, losing some, I asked myself the question, "How can I be better?" I wanted to win more games, so I studied chess moves to improve myself. I noticed that some people had more money than others, not one but two cars, not one but two houses. I wondered how they did that. The only answer I could come up with was that they were better at doing something. So whatever I was doing I just had to get better at it.

Which was, in a nutshell, my solution to the SolidSmack problem. We were at the to-be-or-not-to-be stage. If we wanted to be, then botObjects would just have to be better. We would solve all the technical problems at the front end and eradicate inefficiencies at the back end. We would all have to work even harder—and build a better printer. Then we would deserve to live.

If God is a projection of our own energy, then there should be many gods, a god in everything, and in everyone (or nearly everyone), a god of the volcano, a god of the river, and a god of the mountain.

So I shake out at a kind of optimistic pantheist in the end. If I prayed at all during the botObjects saga, it would have been something like, "Please, great god of business, don't let us die! (Or let down the customers either.)"

19

PUTTING IT IN THE BOX

And the "Destroyer of the Day" award goes to . . .

You know how you order that expensive bit of equipment (let's say, a record player) and it finally arrives and you open the box and . . . it's broken? The tone arm has snapped off or the turntable doesn't turn? You know it's never going to work, and you just have to shove it all back in the box and return to sender?

Well, we're no different. We, at botObjects, are not unbreakable. In fact there's a ton more things to go wrong with a ProDesk3D printer than with most kinds of equipment you might want to buy. There's the nozzle, the rods, the platform going up and down: every single part of the machine is fragile. You might sometimes want to protest about all the packaging—where is all this rubbish going to end up? But—as I well know—you complain even more loudly when your brand-new printer doesn't print.

Of the first ten we sent out six or seven came back. Wrecked. They had to be taken apart and stuck back together again. We had hundreds of orders, but we couldn't get them out, not in one piece. Brushed aluminum, I started to realize, though it certainly looked good, was not the strongest of materials.

There is an art—a science—to packaging. Broadly speaking, the more complicated the tech the better the box you're going to need. We tried all sorts: corrugated, grooved, sculpted. Layer upon layer of cushioning. Paper, cardboard, foam. Triangles, squares, polygons and parallelepipeds. We had to buy bigger, fatter boxes to accommodate all the protection we came up with. And still our printers broke. We drafted in a specialist box maker. Cost us a shedload of money. Still our printers arrived at their destination in more pieces than they set out.

Then Tom—never one to flip—finally flipped. "I've had it with that bloody packaging!" For Tom that was pretty dramatic. He drew the line in the sand that day. At last, I thought. Tom will fix it. I had complete confidence in Tom. He had proved time and time again that there wasn't a single problem he couldn't overcome. He renovated the packaging from top to bottom: new materials, new geometry. His calculations were irrefutable. But of course the only serious test is to replicate the worst you can imagine being done to our poor little printers.

If you want to see how bad it can get you only have to go along to any airport and watch the baggage handlers in action. The question I want to ask is, do they get any training to do this? It makes no odds to them that you have put stickers galore on your box marked "FRAGILE." They chuck them about in a spirit of reckless abandon. No, it's worse than that: I think they actually want to hear the tinkle of breaking technology, like they have a competition going on for the title of "Destroyer of the Day." They seem to be born vandals who have managed to worm their way into the baggage-handling industry, like KGB officers posing as good American citizens in Washington and poised to guide in the next wave of nuclear missiles.

Come the day of the "drop test." The drop test required us to act like JFK baggage handlers. The fact is these boxes were pretty heavy, around fifty-five pounds. Tom and I had to team up to lift one of them over our heads. If you fused us into one, we were like an Olympic weight lifter, doing a clean and jerk, and keeping the bar up at maximum extension for around three seconds. And then we chucked it down.

No noise from the box. Promising. But when we opened the box, lo and behold, there was the nozzle detached from the printer.

Either that or it was the platform. Or something. There was always at least one thing that didn't survive the drop test. Tom admitted defeat. He was fallible after all. He had given it his best shot. So we handed the problem over to Gary at the factory. Surely Gary would fix it, once and for all. Wouldn't he?

"I've solved it," he said, phoning Tom a few weeks later.

"Thank God for that," says Tom.

"It was obvious, really. You just needed a few more polystyrene corners."

"Of course," said Tom. "More polystyrene corners. Should've thought of that."

He sought me out in my office. "M! It's sorted. Gary fixed it. Polystyrene corners, that's all it needed."

"I knew good old Gary would get it done," said I. "He's such a hero. We should have given it to him in the first place instead of all this faffing around. No offense."

Tom was always willing to give someone else the credit. "Lesson learned. Leave it to Gary."

So we headed to New Brunswick. Gary had a more scientific style of drop test than we had had. He actually had a small crane rigged up. We duly attached the box to a pulley at the business end of a long robot arm and stood well back, as if fireworks were about to be let off. Gary pressed a button and like one of those mini-cranes in an amusement arcade that scoops up coins or sweets, the giant maw swooped down and clawed up our little printer. Then it gradually climbed up, hoisting our ProDesk3D with it. At its highest elevation it would have been around twelve feet high. The printer box was swinging in the air. Almost like a man at the end of a noose.

Then Gary pressed the button. The maw released its captive. The box crashed to the ground. With a tragic smashing, shattering noise.

You could see what had happened. Gary really had fixed the problem at the top of the box where most of the damage was occurring. But he'd forgotten all about the bottom. The bottom of the box was crumpled, crushing the delicate contents within. Tom and I were silent. Gary looked at us. "Back to the drawing board, then," he said, phlegmatically. "You need failure. Failure can be good."

Normally I might have agreed with him. It was a Professor-type thing to say. But I wasn't feeling too professorial right then. "Gary, the thing is, we've had failure. We've had nothing but failure. We've got failure coming out of our fucking ears! We could do with a fucking win for a change. Do you think we could do that?"

"Yeah, yeah, a win, I hear you. We can do that."

And the fact is Gary did give us a win—in the end. The answer was inflated plastic. He packed that box with so much inflated plastic the box was more like a balloon. Let the guys at JFK or Heathrow toss it around—it would simply float gently to the floor. After eight or nine iterations of the packaging, we started delivering printers with a high degree of confidence that they would arrive intact at their destination.

Sometimes you need time to get it right. The problem was that we were doing everything with our pedal to the metal.

Then, on the other hand, there was Tokyo (or "Toky-oh-oh" as it became known on campus).

20

HARA-KIRI

Avoid lying at all costs as this almost guarantees customer dissatisfaction. (The Professor, secret #39)

The Tokyo Design Show: It was like the CES (Consumer Electronics Show) of the East. A big deal, in other words. An open sesame to the Asian market. We sent out a press release saying we were scaling up. I saw Tom off on the plane. About twelve hours later I was yelling down the phone. "You only took one fucking printer!? You moron!"

"I couldn't find another one that worked," he replied, meekly.

The printer, to be fair to Tom, had been thoroughly fine-tuned, checked, and calibrated to the millimeter. Then armed with reinforced rubber corners. And assorted inflatables. It went through oversize luggage, marked "FRAGILE" and "DELICATE" and "THIS WAY UP." It should have been idiot-proof. Turns out that the Tokyo baggage handlers are the worst or, depending on how you look at it, the best at smashing your baggage. Tom could actually see them through the window at the airport chucking stuff about like they were playing Frisbee. The box came off the conveyor belt upside down. When he got to his hotel and opened up, he was horrified: both the nozzle and the door were bent or broken. But my simple point was that if he had taken two with him, he could have cannibalized.

"And now the last remaining fully functional ProDesk3D has died. RIP. We tell everyone we are scaling up and we can't get a single effing printer to work? We might as well commit ritual hara-kiri in front of the crowds, they'll probably respect that more."

"Don't you need some kind of traditional Japanese sword for that purpose?"

"Tom, it's a fucking figure of speech! Just sit tight, don't do anything, I'll work something out."

I sent some replacement parts and told Tom to put our appearance at the show on hold for a day or two. The Design Show was spread over several days. I phoned Hiroshi, our Japanese distributor, and told him that we wanted to build up the mystique, so we didn't want to show all our cards too soon. It was all part of the strategy. It was the best excuse I could come up with at the time.

"You are wise, Martin," he said. "We are so excited that you have chosen to honor Japan with your product. We need your printer. With this we will turn around economy." After meteoric growth and industrialization over several decades, Japan had had flat GDP for the last twenty years. It had plateaued out and—even allowing for a certain amount of flowery rhetoric from Hiroshi—he seemed to be counting on botObjects to change the fortunes of the entire nation.

And yet we couldn't find a single working printer. We were supposed to be their lifeline, and we were sinking like a stone. "Yes," said I, instinctively bowing over the phone. "It will be our pleasure and our privilege."

"This is going to be great," he said. "A breakthrough. Everything rests on Tokyo Design Show."

"No problem," said I, echoing Dylan.

Tom, meanwhile, was keeping his head down, licking his wounds at his hotel. There was nothing he could do until the replacement parts turned up. We were dependent on FedEx. I had to keep on blagging it over the phone. Not lying, mind you—I hate to know-ingly lie—but possibly getting a little bit creative. ("Avoid lying at all costs as this almost guarantees customer dissatisfaction"—Secret #39, *The Entrepreneur's Book of Secrets*).

"We will be ready."

"I'm not sure when we will be doing the press show."

"You'll have to ask Tom—he's the man in situ."

"Tom must be out enjoying all the delights of Tokyo. He told me he wanted to visit a Zen garden. He loves azaleas." I mean, who doesn't love azaleas?

I couldn't dial Tom's number fast enough after I put the phone down to Hiroshi. "He's calling you right now. He thinks it's all going to be great. We're supposed to be saving Japan."

"How can we do that?"

"By getting the fucking printer working!"

But FedEx were not helping. They didn't deliver that day or the next. We would have to go public with the news. There was no way around it. We had blown it. Again. But I would have to let Hiroshi know first.

"I'm so sorry man, it's not working, it got smashed at the airport. It's imperfect. It's fragile. What can I tell you? I wanted to bring you into the circle of trust."

Hiroshi went quiet for a moment. "Martin, can I help?"

"How do you mean?"

"We have spare parts here, in Tokyo."

"You do?"

"Martin, the more you say it's imperfect but we have repaired it, the more we like it and believe in it. We don't believe perfect."

"OK, well, the nozzle is bent and the door is broken."

Hiroshi wanted us to come to the rescue of Japan; but the real-ity was that Hiroshi came to our rescue. He delivered the parts to Tom and Tom stuck it all together with surgical precision. The printer was finally unveiled at the Tokyo Design Show. One fully operational ProDesk3D at the botObjects stand. It looked good, and it worked.

And there was a long, snaking queue of people lining up to have a gander at it.

Hiroshi remained our most trusted distributor around the world. It was one of those rare and heartwarming cases of a transnational collaboration saving the day. I was always reminded, in thinking of Hiroshi, of the great Japanese tradition of kintsugi, where they take some precious and fragile piece of pottery—a bowl or a vase—that has been accidentally broken and restore it, even enhance it, using a golden glue.

On the whole I'd rather that than hara-kiri. And Hiroshi and I remain firm friends to this day, held together by the golden glue of botObjects.

21

THE BACKUP PLAN

How to outfox Fox

I was amazed when I got the callback. I honestly thought once was enough. But if they wanted to do it all over again. . . . And Stuart Varney was his old charming self. How could I say no? There was one big difference. This time Fox Business News wanted to show our printer printing live on TV. This was a first for them. And for us.

No robots! That was something. All the same, need I say that yours truly was panicking. Big-time. And for once cool-as-a-cucumber Tom was panicking just as much as I was. And cussing too, which was rare for him. "On live TV? Are you fucking crazy? That's not going to happen."

The whole company was working overtime to try and get everything ready for the big night (or rather morning). We ended up the night before the big day with one very suave-looking printer that was pimped and primed. We had a plan too, to print something small (how about a key ring, for example?) but also distinctive for just this purpose (I know, why don't we print the word "FOX" on it?). There was only one thing: we had absolutely no idea if it was going to work in front of the cameras.

I remembered what those cameras were like. They were huge for one thing. With several lenses poking out of them like bazookas. They were meant to be scarily invasive—like Daleks—Exterminate! And I couldn't help but feel our poor little printer was going to be exposed in the cruel light of the studio as a . . . no, not a "fake" or a "scam" or any of those nasty things that had been said about us, but yes, perhaps as a fallible and unreliable piece of work that could break down or produce the wrong colors or the wrong shape or have some kind of meltdown at practically any time of day or night. Which would be worse because it was real.

That was the fun thing about the ProDesk3D—it was as unpredictable as a particularly random quantum particle. Call it mercurial if you will. Moody. With a fair wind, it could be great, it could be world-beating, it could be beautiful, it could be a Mona Lisa among printers—or it could be a total, sickening dud. It was just impossible to know on any given day. We were like one of those brilliant soccer teams of whom it is sometimes said, derisively, *they just didn't turn up!* What were the chances of us turning up and doing the job? I would give it no better than 50/50. I wouldn't bet the house on it.

I was pacing up and down trying to work out some kind of backup plan. Maybe we should just call the whole thing off? The upside was good, but the potential downside of a full-on fiasco was too dreadful to contemplate. The first Fox interview had been nothing but productive for us and had pulled in customers and distributors and would-be investors (we turned down millions). The second Fox interview could make us—or, all too likely, break us. For once the risk outweighed the reward.

"Don't worry about it," says Tom. "I've got us covered."

"How do you mean, covered?"

"I've been practicing."

"Practicing what exactly?" All I wanted was infallibility and, if possible, omniscience. Was that too much to ask for?

"Watch."

Tom showed me a key ring he had printed out earlier, one with the FOX name all over it in upper case. Perfect. "Yeah, but . . . " I said. We had to print live this time, not turn up with something we printed out earlier.

"Hold on."

He went over to the printer and took out his phone and tapped out some instructions.

The printer started rolling.

Tom jabbed his phone a second time. The printer stopped.

"Oops," says he. "It seems to have paused. Let me have a look . . ."

He stuck his hand into the platform and waved it around and then pulled it out. And in his hand he had: the FOX key ring. Somehow he had made the indeterminate piece of nothing—like a lump of mold—that had originally sat there disappear and conjured up the key ring in his place. It was a piece of stage magic worthy of David Copperfield. "I used to do magic tricks," he said. "Making coins appear and disappear. Pulling flowers out of hats. I got to be quite good at it. I never did rabbits, I didn't think it would be fair to rabbits. But I thought it might come in handy tomorrow."

Tom had completely fooled me. Perhaps he could outfox those Fox cameras too? It was worth a shot—I had nothing.

The next day at the studio, as usual they had all the delicious snacks in the greenroom. And free drinks too. The sad thing is that we were too nervous to enjoy any of the perks. They had the printer running for most of the show off-set, and would keep on turning back to the shot of it beavering away, then we were finally ushered in to Room 101 toward the end to see if it had worked or not. We were the climax of the show. Let's face it, they were probably hoping for blood on the floor—made it more fun for viewers, I imagine. I was sweating bricks. I imagine they felt like this when they were being marched up to the guillotine.

We had set up the printer with a little curtain in front of it, so that nobody would be able to see what was produced before the job was finished (and, of course, it would also potentially spare our blushes if the machine blew it). Tom switched it off and reached behind the curtain. His hand emerged with a newly printed FOX key ring in it. I took it from him and handed it to Stuart.

"I'm not allowed to accept gifts, you know," he said.

"Stuart, it's a key ring for goodness sake. Made of plastic. It's all we could do in the time. I doubt they'll lock you up for taking it."

Tom and I regrouped in the taxi. "Well?" I said.

He smiled enigmatically.

"Did it work or didn't it?" I really needed to know.

Tom looked at me and tapped a finger to his nose. "A magician never gives away his secrets."

To this day I don't know if Tom swapped the key rings or not. It didn't matter. After the show aired, demand exploded. But then demand had never been a problem: it had already hit the ceiling, now it went through the roof. Supply, however, was another matter again.

22

THE BIT I NEARLY MISSED OUT

"It is not unusual for the entrepreneur to get despondent."

I almost forgot to mention this. In fact I deliberately didn't mention it. Because, to be honest, I feel ashamed even now. Especially about the recorder. It was the one time I really flipped my lid (well, maybe not the one and only). A lot of hand-waving, cursing, probably some inadvertent saliva flying around. You can imagine—the works. My only excuse: the pressure. We were on a deadline and Tom starts mucking about—or at least, that's the way I saw it at the time.

We need to rewind twenty-four hours, to the day before the show. Tom flew over and joined me in New Jersey.

I put him up at a hotel close to my house (out of the way of the kids). Or, okay, motel. It wasn't quite the Norman Bates motel, and I didn't see any rats running around inside. But for sure there were a few outside, and I guess you could call it homely. Or possibly a health hazard. But either way he ended up in a rather poky, dismal room with—of course—a printer for company.

All the same, the night before the big show we were in an upbeat mood. Confident. Call it hubris if you will. We had it all under control.

Tom and I were like a like a pilot and copilot going through the checks before takeoff:

Power unit, check.

Leveling platform, check.

Temperature, check.

Our baby was tested and certified healthy and 100 percent. We had done our homework. There would be no turbulence and no risk of crashing. Would there? We had the plan. We had the backup plan. Twenty-five to thirty minutes to print the key ring. No worries. No need to stress out. The Fox show was life or death, but we were prepared for every eventuality. So of course we went and had a few beers. Relax and unwind. What could go wrong?

There happened to be a bar in the hotel. "What's your local beer?" asks Tom. That was a sure sign his confidence was high. He's a bit of a beer connoisseur. When he's worried he'll order a diet coke. We had a couple of "Brown Bears." Tom approved so he had a couple more.

"Big day tomorrow!" I said when we went our separate ways.

"Balls to the wall!" says he, jovially, raising a glass. Not an expression I really get, but it sounded positive. We'd had a few, so I was not overly concerned with semantics at this point. I left him ordering another, bartender please.

CUT TO: The following morning. Not quite the crack of dawn. I gave it till around 8 a.m. before calling. Tom was not answering his phone. So I went over to his hotel/motel and hung around in reception for a while, drinking their free coffee (which is all they offered by way of breakfast). Then I went up and knocked on his door.

I'm not saying Tom had a hangover, but he might as well have had one. His hair was as spiky as a Sputnik, he was unshaven, and he looked as if he hadn't slept all night. Not a good sign. Not Fox camera-worthy. Maybe a stand-in for *The Hangover*.

"You look like shit, mate," I said.

"I've lost it," he said.

"I can see that."

"No, I mean I've lost the key ring."

I felt like a cold hand had reached into me and clutched my vitals. But I tried to keep it under control. "How can you 'lose' it? It's a key ring—it's so you don't lose your keys."

"I don't know what happened," he said, running a hand through his increasingly chaotic hair. "One moment I had it and the next it was gone."

"Have you looked . . . ?"

He nodded. He had already looked everywhere. Clearly this line of questioning was not going anywhere.

"OK," says I, philosophically. "Let's just print another one, shall we? Then we have backup. Isn't that the great thing about having a super cool 3D printer? Any time anywhere you can just print whatever you need. What are we even worrying about?"

I think I may have managed a slightly nervous laugh. But there was something about Tom's drawn and haggard face that choked off my merriment.

"About that . . ." he said.

"Are you telling me . . .?"

"Yeah."

"You fucking moron." I wasn't cool, calm, and philosophical any more. Now I had "lost it" too. It was a pressure situation. Because the thing he was telling me without actually telling me was that the printer had stopped working. The way it always did, given long enough. Let me say straight away that the barrage of insults directed at Tom was completely unfair and unjustified. It was the printer that was at fault, not Tom (although, having said that, he could at least have not lost the bloody key ring as well). The printer, although beautiful, was a temperamental Marilyn Monroe among printers: You never knew if she was going to turn up on the day or had not learned her lines or, on any given day, whether a complete meltdown was on the cards. If it wasn't one thing it was another. We had not just three fans but twelve motors. And a nozzle that was supposed to spit out a rainbow. There was so much scope for things to go wrong.

The night before we were flying high. A few hours later we had crashed and burned.

Which I hope helps to explain exactly why I was panicking and blowing my top. We had pinned all our hopes and dreams to a machine that was as flaky and precarious as a broken helicopter clinging to the edge of a cliff in a *Mission: Impossible* movie. Without Tom Cruise to come and save us we were sunk.

8. Entrepreneur Mindset
It is not unusual for the entrepreneur to get despondent (says the Professor), since in the beginning many things can go wrong, and it's easy to get discouraged. For example, the product isn't fully tested or requires more work than expected, or the startup isn't growing as fast as anticipated. Entrepreneurs can start to experience self-doubt.

You (or I) can say that again. And now the clock was ticking. We had those Fox cameras ready to eat us up and spew us out and distributors flying in to ask for their money back. I could already hear those dreaded TV studio words: "You're on!"

I marched up and down the threadbare rug on the floor a few times and metaphorically punched a few holes in the (already pockmarked) wall.

"I printed a recorder," Tom said.

"What!?" What was he going on about?

"Look," he said. He went and picked up the recorder. It looked like a tube of multicolored Life Savers stuck end to end. You couldn't call it beautiful, but it was spectacular.

I gritted my teeth. "A penny whistle!" I exclaimed. "That's about all this printer is worth—a penny! I bet it doesn't even work."

Tom responded by putting the business end to his lips and blew. A few squeaky notes came out. "It works!" he said, prancing up and down like a Morris dancer.

"No, it doesn't," I said, grabbing the recorder from his hands and snapping it in two over my knee (just as I once had with my headmaster's cane). Cruel I know, but if Tom hadn't messed around making the recorder the printer would still be working. I went over to a bin in the corner of the room and chucked the pieces in. "You fucked up."

Breaking something, as it happened, was just what I needed. It enabled me to let some steam out. I basically wanted to pick that printer up and smash the bastard down on the ground and give its broken corpse a bloody good kicking. But the recorder was a good substitute or scapegoat. Shame though. It was probably one of the best things we had ever done, there was no other printer in the world that could produce anything like that. Tom had topped the pink whistle. And now I had destroyed it.

Tom looked distraught.

"OK, so what's wrong with the bloody printer?" I said, trying to focus and get us back on track.

"The print isn't sticking," says Tom and gave me a demo.

Remember that the way the printer works is to heap up layer upon layer to create the object, very thin layers, almost like layers of paint that merge into one another so (ideally) you can't see the joins. But on this morning of mornings, right before the big Fox interview, the layers were peeling. We had quite literally come unstuck. When it worked, it was almost like magic. When it didn't, you ended up with a pile of frozen plastic that was about as useful as a melted candle.

"We are so fucking toast!" I said it with more sadness than anything. I wasn't fuming, I wasn't going through the roof, I was more on the verge of tears. I remember a show in which a so-called "cyber-truck" was being demo'd. The main point about the cyber-truck was that it was immune to villains breaking into it and stealing stuff or making off with the vehicle itself. It was supposedly bulletproof. "Look," said a certain self-important (and overly self-confident) CEO behind the cyber-truck. "I can take this sledgehammer and smash it against the driver's window and it won't break." Smiling for the camera, he picked up his handy sledgehammer, swung it—and the window shattered.

Oops. The cyber-truck had been exposed as a flop. Live, on air. That's exactly what I foresaw happening to us.

"I think I know what the problem is," says Tom.

Something was off, by a fraction—the speed, the rate, the temperature. The leveling platform wasn't level or the scanner wasn't scanning or the filaments weren't feeding—or all of the above. He's not Tom Cruise, but Tom is a genius when it comes to practical engineering. Somehow, he (in conjunction with Gaston over the phone) managed to dig us out of a very deep hole, and we made it on time to the Fox studio and we survived torture by TV yet again, by the skin of our teeth.

This is how it always was with the ProDesk3D—it was like playing chutes and ladders, with our fleeting moments of triumph invariably cut short by another sudden descent into crisis. Somehow we came through.

Whatever, I still feel bad about breaking Tom's recorder. And Tom: please delete some of my more colorful vocabulary from your memory banks.

23

THE INTERN

The problem of excess viscosity

His name was Theo. He was probably our youngest ever intern (i.e., we weren't paying him a dime). He wasn't even technically an intern; he was doing "work experience" as part of his school curriculum. Somebody had recommended him to somebody. Theo was only a long-haired, bespectacled fifteen-year-old at the time this happened (but the kind of kid who could "jailbreak" his own phone—or yours— and no doubt hack into the Pentagon in his spare time).

Declaration of interest: he was also my son.

I was just coming back to the office from seeing lawyers and, as usual, the printer wasn't working. "It doesn't work, Tom!" I said for the umpteenth time, verging on despair, praying for the ground to open up and swallow both me and the printer so this nonfunctional night-mare could finally be over. It was my default position. "The fucking printer's not working!" I don't know how many times I said this. A lot.

We were in the War Room. I remember there were some horses going by outside, clip-clopping along. This was our "campus." It was a tranquil, pastoral scene—outside. Inside, we had cooked up a Darth

Vader helmet. Multicolor of course. Looked like a big ice-cream. Which might not have suited Darth himself. And it would have been a bit on the small size too. But the real problem was that it wasn't cooling properly. It wasn't "curing." It was more like a melting tub of ice cream. It was cold on the outside, but it must still be hot on the inside. Could it be one of the fans wasn't working?

At this point I was yelling at Tom and/or the fans. Tom was on his computer, working through a simulation, trying to figure out what was going on, or not going on. "Don't worry, I'll work it out," he said, with his usual bluff and bravado. He must have told me not to worry about one thousand times, but someone had to.

Theo took no notice of us. He was tinkering with the machine. I don't know where the kid got it from, but it was like the machine spoke to his soul. He was some kind of 3D printer–whisperer. He had already printed out some multicolor bracelets to mystify his schoolmates and annoy his teachers. "The fans are operational," he said. "But the air is not being distributed evenly around the object. It's not a problem if the object is big. But it becomes a factor if it's small."

Theo was in tenth grade at school. He was a tall, gangly kid with John Lennon glasses. But he spoke like some old professor. "It's a fluid dynamics problem. As you can see, the object has excess viscosity." He didn't say the "helmet" or Darth Vader or anything. I'm not sure he had even seen *Star Wars*. He was probably too busy reading his science textbooks.

I admit: I had to look up "viscosity." I thought he was making it up. This boy will go far, I thought to myself. "I don't get it. What difference should it make if we print it this big or that big?" I always tried to speak politely to the younger generation: I didn't want to be a bad influence on anyone. (Someone like Tom was beyond being influenced one way or another.)

"It's your tri-fan architecture," he said. Naturally, I had given Theo an intro to some of the printer's most distinctive features. "You've got the top fan in the wrong place. It's not cooling the smaller objects."

I refused to believe. The tri-fan architecture was my baby. It couldn't be wrong—could it? Theo started printing something to demonstrate the point. But Tom was listening, and he ran some permutations through his simulator. "He's right," says Tom. "Bang on. Theo just worked out what we have been knocking ourselves out over."

"Are you sure?"

The printer was still clacking away. "The numbers don't lie. We have to reposition." Tom paused to look admiringly at Theo. "This kid is better than me!" The funny thing was, Tom sounded happy about it, as if he couldn't wait to pass on the baton to the next generation.

"If you weren't still at school," I said to him, "we would definitely hire you."

We took Theo out for a Coke and a pizza, on the house. With fries on the side. He looked as if he could do with feeding up. He eyed up the chips as if he was going to give advice to the chef on how to improve the oven.[4]

---

4   Theo is now in industrial design, specializing in aviation—and working for me, full-time.

24

APOCALYPSE NOW

Size is everything

This was our basic problem. We were designing from the outside in; we should have been designing from the inside out. But we were prioritizing form. And Tom was pulling another all-nighter. Which did not go down well with the Colonel.

The Colonel was our landlord. We were working in what was in essence a farmhouse. To picture our campus, you have to realize one big thing, or possibly two big things: On the inside, we were trying to bring the future forward; on the outside, they were trying to bring back the past. We were at the cutting edge of capitalism; they were the robust holdouts of feudalism. And "they" in this case were embodied by the Colonel.

The Colonel was a grouchy, abrasive, shaven-headed, and still very fit seventy-year-old who had once served in the US military in far-flung campaigns in which he almost certainly had to "destroy" certain villages in order to "save" them. In looks he reminded me of Robert Duvall in *Apocalypse Now*. I could well imagine him expressing a fondness for the smell of napalm in the morning. He had since morphed into a country squire in Upstate New York and rented out some of the properties on his estate as, nominally, a "science park." It was still more park than science. There were stables nearby, and horses would regularly clop along past our office. It made me feel we—the whole botObjects crew—were in a time machine and had landed here from the future. From the Colonel's point of view, we were now part of the military-industrial complex, with the emphasis on military. With the appropriate level of discipline.

The Colonel and his wife interviewed me when I applied for the lease on the farmhouse to check if they liked the cut of my jib. I had to smarten up and put on a tie and be on my best behavior just to get through the door of his elegant eighteenth-century colonial house. His wife served tea and cupcakes in fine china cups and plates. He wanted to know where I had gone to school and what I did for a living. "I'm an entrepreneur," I said. "An innovator."

"Good," he said, doubtfully.

"We're a startup—building a new 3D printer."

"Excellent." He tended to talk in these one-word sentences, pre-sumably on a par with the orders he used to give: "March!" "Fire!" And so on. He didn't sound too enthusiastic, but he leased us the farmhouse anyway.

If he was the squire, we were the peasants. If he was commander in chief, we were foot soldiers. Naturally, he moaned and fussed about everything. One day, one of our staff parked his car over an imaginary line and he blew his top. Which was mad considering it was a field, not a parking lot. But it was Tom who most often incurred his wrath. Tom was trying to work out the size problem. The ProDesk3D had, as the name implied, to fit on your desk. So it had to be small. On the other hand it had to accommodate an awful lot of hardware—all those cartridges and motors and tubes—to be the all-singing, all-dancing piece of hi-tech that it undoubtedly was. Which meant that, in effect, the printer was being pulled every which way in size like a multidi-mensional accordion. And when you changed the size you changed everything. The specifications remained unspecified. So often enough

Tom had to slog through the night and sleep, if he slept at all, on the sofa. And you would find him in the morning unkempt and unshaven and un-everything you might want in a well-turned-out, presentable G.I. Joe. There was just something about him that seemed to rile our landlord. Or possibly everything.

One morning the Colonel marched in. He had a habit of just walking in, unannounced. By chance, we happened to be playing foosball at the time. Needless to say, he didn't approve. "Lights!" he barked. "Security!" We knew what he was going on about. He didn't like the premises being occupied and therefore illuminated through the night. It was odd because if anything it improved security. Surely if it was unoccupied it would be more of a target? But none of my most cogent arguments, or Tom's, carried any weight with him. "Time!" "Money!"

It wasn't until that one sunny morning, with the aroma of freshly brewed coffee hanging in the air and Gaston bearing croissants, that the Colonel's defenses finally (if briefly) crumbled. You won't find croissants in every café in the United States, but Gaston had taken to bringing in croissants regularly because he felt we needed the civilizing French (or at least French-Canadian) influence. He threatened, playing up to his stereotype, to bring in snails to eat too, but fortunately that never came to pass.

We were amazed when the Colonel took up his offer of a croissant and proceeded to dunk it in his coffee too. Except he called it "café au lait" with a French accent that Gaston approved of and didn't sound anything like Robert Duvall. Gaston put up a passionate defense of what we were up to. "This may not be cold fusion," he says (not sure the Colonel would have known what that was anyway), "but one is innovating. We are inventing every single day. C'est génial."

"Magnifique!" beamed the Colonel, immediately on the French wavelength.

There was something about Gaston and his croissants that had softened him. I like to think that he'd once been in love with Brigitte Bardot—or someone of her era in Paris or perhaps on one of his foreign campaigns—and still carried a torch. Maybe he had done a stint in the Foreign Legion? Either way he remained grumpy, but from then on I think I understood his pain. Love or war, heartbreak comes with the territory.

25

SUPPLY AND DEMAND

"It is clear that great entrepreneurs have a plan on how to approach supply and demand, but the initial steps are taken to create or secure the supply side."

I can remember seeing a graph in my Economics 101 textbook showing supply and demand perfectly aligned. In "equilibrium." Straight lines cutting perfect diagonals across the page and intersecting bang in the middle. Beautifully symmetrical. But that is geometry for you. Reality is never like that, alas. The worst thing is when supply is greater than demand: you made it, and now no one wants it. Tough. But almost as bad, in my humble experience, is when demand outstrips supply: you haven't made it, but everyone wants it. That's the situation we were in at botObjects. We were about a million miles from attaining perfect equilibrium and tranquility.

And then the price went up.

I remember getting the call from Gary. I happened to be in a particularly optimistic mood, oddly enough. It was a lovely sunny day and I was on my second cup of coffee. "Morning all!" says I, walking through the door. "How's it going?" Smiles and "Fine!" all round.

Everything was looking good. The media were writing about us almost every day, but by and large in a good way. We had solved all the major technical problems (and I'm sorry if I've said that before—but we really had this time!) The naysayers were in full retreat. Eden was going great guns with the marketing. Distributors had agreed to call off the hit men for now. The ProDesk3D was going to be solid gold. We were flying.

And then the wings dropped off.

Jack said to give Gary a call.

"What's he want?"

"Better call him and find out." That was the sound of Jack chickening out.

So I called him straight back. "Hey, Gary, how's it, my man?" I was still in my breezy confidence mood.

"We've got to change suppliers," says Gary. "For the motors."

"What's wrong with the old suppliers?" The old suppliers were in China, which kept the costs down.

"They're not exactly saying, but I heard a rumor their CEO just got arrested."

I didn't like the sound of a CEO getting arrested. "OK . . ." Breezy was fast giving way to anxious.

"I've got to make another mold."

"What's wrong with the old mold?"

"You changed the door."

"We changed the color, Gary, not the shape."

"Anyway, what with one thing and another the price is going to have to—"

"Don't say it, Gary!" I'd done with anxiety, I was moving on to panic.

"—go—"

"Gary! Gary! Hold on."

"—up."

Sometimes the word "up" can be a total downer. Pricing was always going to be a sensitive point. For one thing, if you want to go right back to the beginning, we had taken on something we knew little about. Then we had fixed on a price without having a proper bill of materials. We had picked the $3k mark out of a hat and hoped; it was right at the top end of the consumer market. We couldn't go much over that without choking off demand. So Gary had just blown a great big hole right through my sunny mood of cheerfulness. Basically, he was stiffing us, inflating his margin at our expense.

Meanwhile, in the background, I had all those vultures—a.k.a. distributors—circling overhead and making regular calls. "How many units and when?" "Why can't you produce more?" "But you promised me fifteen printers!" Generally I relied on Jack to take the calls, but every now and then he would let them filter through to me so I could feel his pain. "Mexico wants out!"

It's funny how sometimes a day that starts out so bright and sunny can get dark and stormy. The reality principle had kicked in, the way it always does. And now we were about to lose our margin. Our margin was already marginal. Gary was threatening to put the cost to us up by around a grand. We were caught between a rock and a hard place. This was all on one day, by the way. Gary squeezing us and distributors walking out and asking for their money back.

"Gary, we've got to stay within margin."

"I can't do it at cost."

"Can't you find cheaper suppliers?"

"Everybody wants cheaper. We found the cheapest, and now they're toast. Maybe they were too cheap?"

Then it was back on the phone to our French distributor. He was into it for half a million. I remember he used the word *merde* a lot. Apparently shops wanted their money back. "It's got all these advanced features—that's what's caused the delay. No problem with refunding if you want to walk away. But we are changing the world."

I was probably on my sixth coffee of the day when I had an idea.

"Hey Gary, you know that giga factory you were talking about?" It was his big dream.

"Yeah."

"I reckon if we can keep the cost down on this one we could be looking at investing in that in the future. What do you think?"

"I think the giga factory is the next step for sure. Expand production and lower costs. It's logical."

"Maybe we can just keep costs on a level for now?"

Gary was always straight with us. But he was also crafty. I knew he would have a contingency up his sleeve. Or if he didn't he would conjure one up.

"Gary on the phone for you," says Jack toward the end of the day.

We were back on. I knew he would find a backup, whether it was motors or mold. "Gary, my man, what's new?"

Every day was a bit like that—juggling with about ten plates in the air. I was in a constant state of high anxiety, yo-yoing from high to low and then back up again. It was worse than being in love. But it was like Leonardo DiCaprio said: You're here because you want to be.

26

THE IMPOSSIBLE DREAM

In which we see a canoid patch of color

The fact is the Colonel didn't approve of pets, but we sold it to him as a guard dog. Or dogs.

I don't know exactly why I took Cujo with me to campus on that particular day. I think it had something to do with the snow. Or perhaps my mental state was so precarious that I really needed a dog with me by way of moral support. Or was it pure, unadulterated luck?

I know this is going to sound mad, but we actually have seven dogs, my wife and I. Sometimes it seems like more. There are dogs every-where, running around in the garden, hanging about in the kitchen, snoozing on the sofa or a bed somewhere, generally ruling the roost. It's not "our house," it's more like a doghouse, staffed by a couple of human servants. How did this come about? Like most things, it was more by chance than design. We started off with just the one, Spot, a sweet-natured poodle. Then Cupcake, a bouncy spaniel bitch, came along, inherited from a distant relative. We should have antici-pated that Cupcake might become pregnant. And go on to have four beautiful hybrid pups, "cockapoos," in an array of colors, from honey to treacle. And we found homes for all four of them. But when it came to the crunch we could never bear to part with any of them. I suppose giving them all names—Gobi, Lion, Cujo, and Aloo—didn't help. One time a long-time housekeeper was leaving to get married and we all agreed she should have Aloo, our littlest one. We got as far as putting Aloo in the car with her, but before she could drive away we rushed out and took him back again. He looked happy to come and join his mates. Oh, yes, not forgetting Lola—sister to Cupcake and auntie to all the pups—came to join them when she heard it was a regular riot at our place. Hence seven. (And in case you're wondering, yes, this time we have taken precautions, so seven is our maximum canine occupancy.)

So anyway on this particular day, with the snow in Upstate New York at least a foot deep, I took Cujo into work with me. Cujo (named after the friendly Saint Bernard who goes mad in the Stephen King horror flick of that name) is just a classic doggy dog, with curly brown hair, medium-sized, with a sunny disposition, who loves to play with humans or any other animal. His supreme virtue, from my point of view, is that he is almost entirely indifferent to the 3D printer industry and much more concerned with having regular meals, exercise, and a comfortable bed to curl up in. Not to mention a few friends—and he had plenty of willing walkers at botObjects, even in the snow.

I had almost forgotten, in the midst of one crisis or another, that this was the very same day on which Krystal Williams was due to pay us a visit. On the whole we tried to avoid any major close encounters on campus. If we had meetings or interviews or photoshoots or whatever, we tried to arrange them at the office in New York. We kept that place looking pristine and uncluttered, glossy and glassy, looking as if we really knew what we were doing. Campus, in contrast, was pure improvisation, which is to say chaos by another name. Call it creative chaos if you will. Campus was forever on the verge of a nervous breakdown, but at the same time mostly cheerful and optimistic. Or at least we tried hard to remain optimistic, which is not quite the same thing. For some reason, Krystal Williams insisted on driving out of town to meet us. She preferred face-to-face to over-the-phone. And she wanted to see where the "real work" was done. Thought it would be good for her story, more authentic. She was writing a business profile for her technology blog (which had a lot of followers).

Tom had pulled another all-nighter, making sure that there were at least a couple of fully functioning printers around the place. We felt two were a minimum: she might see through the feeble pretense of a lonely, solo, viable printer. He looked hungover without the benefit of having been to a party, so after a brief intro I moved Krystal smartly on to meet Dylan ("Hi") and Gaston (more conventionally, eloquently charming). Eden took her in hand for a brief tour around the campus. Then she brought her back to me in my office for a longer conversation. Krystal was a thirtysomething native of the Bronx with a degree in journalism from CUNY who had established herself as an "influencer." She wore what looked to my eye like an expensive houndstooth suit, with high heels, and carried a shoulder bag by Coach. But it turned out she was also a dog-lover. And Cujo, in return, loved her.

When the human came in, the dog was curled up peacefully in his bed—with a big juicy bone pattern, I recall—at the side of my desk. "Who is this gorgeous boy?" was the first thing Krystal said. And she wasn't talking about me. Cujo duly bounded up and nuzzled her, wagging not just his tail but his whole body.

"No jumping!" I said, conscious of her immaculate clothes—I didn't want him to inflict his dirty paws on her.

"Awww, let him jump!" says she, starting to dance around the office with him.

For the next half hour or so, I tried to tell her about how revolutionary the ProDesk3D was, how fast it was, how it was full-color etc., and she had her recording device switched on, but she seemed far more interested in what Cujo had to say to her. He was all over her or she was all over him, I'm not sure which. And the piece of information that impressed her the most was not our amazing technical specifications, nor my brilliant career, but rather the simple fact that

I had seven dogs. "That's wonderful," says she. The more the merrier was her opinion. She told me all about her dog too, a French bulldog called Aurora Persephone Nefertiti (and I think there may have been a couple more names) but generally known as Rory for short.

Which explains why she asked if we could print a dog. "Sure," I said. "No problem." Actually, my first thought was that is a problem, but I didn't like to say so.

"Could it be your lovely dog, Cujo?"

"Sure."

Nothing was less sure, but I got Dylan to come in and take some pictures and then convert them into a file and feed it into the printer. "It won't be life-sized exactly."

"Any size would be great."

It was only ever going to be a small one—a bigger one would just have taken too long. But we had caught Cujo in one of his more adorable poses: sitting nicely, but looking up at the camera, curious and alert (head cocked to one side) and full of love for the world. And of course the color was about right, honey with a little bit of treacle here and there.

Krystal loved the 3D dog almost as much as the real thing. "Rory is going to be so pleased to have a little friend," she said. She put the botObject dog in her Coach bag and gave the original Cujo a big farewell hug. Her eventual post raved about how "lifelike" our printed dog was. That was one of our minor triumphs.

I thought to myself when I read her piece that, yes, you could say our creation was lifelike, so long as life was mostly plastic and solid on the inside. The replica Cujo was never going to leap up at you and roll around on the grass or walk down the street, or run, or chase cats or paw and snort at the fresh snow. Maybe we could work on a robot dog that could do all the above (and, ideally, walk in a straight line, unlike Rofi).

But it occurred to me that Spot and Cupcake had done a perfect job of producing a 3D dog (in fact four of them) in the first place. Until we could do that we were only producing cheap, clunky models of the real thing. Copulation still scored over replication. Bertrand Russell once said that, given the risk of uncertainty and potential delusion, you couldn't really say with absolute certitude, "There goes a dog," but only, "I see a canoid patch of color." Well, I had seen a canoid patch of color but I still yearned for the proper dog.

The ultimate, perhaps impossible dream has to be the perfect imitation of the original, all-singing—or barking—all-dancing furry friend. In an ideal world, the 3D-printed simulacrum would be indistinguishable from the original dog. As in a 3D Turing test, you would look from one to the other and you wouldn't know which was which. What I really wanted was a matter transporter—I would have liked to beam up a dog. But at least Krystal was happy with her botObjects Cujo. And, as the Professor would say, "Influencers are themselves searching for great content, there will be lots of ways to engage influencers, and perhaps collaborate for free. This is a great way to get exposure. You may be able to feed a part of their story they want to tell." All we had to do was feed the dog(s).

27

THE ZOMBIE

So is it 3D or 2D?

We had a 3D printer, and we had full color. But did we have 3D full color?

That was the apparently absurd question that, quite unexpectedly, I found myself batting around with Tom. Of course we had full-color 3D printing on our prototypes, as programmed by Gaston and Dylan, where we could manually set the colors. No problem. We had the canoid patch of full color, we had a full-color Eiffel Tower. But when it came to the consumer-level machines, programmed only by amateurs, in their own homes, we didn't.

You couldn't release the printer without the right software, developed by Dylan. But was it right?

"You know we have this deadline approaching, don't you?" I said, one fine day in the New Year. We had orders going through the roof and we had already missed two deadlines and somehow we were still clinging on. One more postponement would probably kill us. Distributors were closing in like a pack of particularly ravenous wolves. Our reputation, such as it was, would be finally shredded. We had a fortnight to deliver on our promises. "Under-promise, over-de-liver": Secret no. 17 of *The Entrepreneur's Book of Secrets*. So far we had got that exactly upside down and backward.

"We'll be ready, M!" said Tom, standing in front of me, and giving me a cheerful salute.

"That's a relief," says I. "I was fearful you were going to muck me about again."

"On the other hand . . ." says he. I hated the other hand. "Ideally, we would have a bit more time."

"Why?"

"There are teething issues."

"Hold on," says I, feeling a queer kind of sickening, crunching, imminent bankruptcy feeling creeping up my spine, "I thought we were 'all set to rock 'n' roll.' Isn't that what you said the other day? What kind of teething issues?"

"Don't worry, we can get the basics out any time." Whenever he came out with his old "Don't worry, be happy" refrain, like a record on repeat, I knew it was time to worry. "We can always do a ProDesk3d 2.0, you know, the next generation, updated, with all the bugs fixed. They all do that, Apple, Google, Samsung."

"So what sort of 'bug' are we talking about here? Specifically?"

"It's just a software problem we've picked up."

"Oh that's all right then!" I admit I was sarcastic and bitter, I guess I'm just that kind of guy. "It's only software—exactly what the customer needs to get the printer working properly. No one ever said about a successful product, hey, it's great—it's just the software doesn't work."

Tom went pale. "It's a detail to do with the color." (I.e., only our biggest selling point.)

I won't say it was like getting blood out of a stone, but sometimes getting Tom to explain the latest problem was like trying to get a 3D printer printing an object on a bad day. Even if it worked it was grindingly, frustratingly slow. "What kind of detail?" That looming bankruptcy feeling had now fully worked its way up my spine and right into what was left of my rapidly melting brain.

"Um," he said. "You know how we have 3D prints?"

"Yes, of course I know that, it's the whole point of it."

"Well, the color is a bit more 2D."

"How do you mean exactly?"

"Well, so far we can only get our software to print color on one side of any object, not all three sides."

"Great!" I said. "I know, why don't we fucking rebrand ourselves as ProDesk2D?"

"We could do that, I suppose," says Tom, utterly immune to irony, no matter how heavy. "But we're working on the other two sides."

"So, if we have a tripod, you can color one of the legs."

"The front of one maybe."

"And if we have a crippled robot you could maybe color its face?" The "crippled" was a harsh comment on Rofi, but not entirely unjustified.

"And the front of his legs!"

At this point the steam was coming out of my ears. "Get fucking Dylan in here!" Dylan was the software supremo. It was his baby and his problem.

Tom went out and brought in Dylan. "No problem," says Dylan.

"What do you mean, you moron, no problem? It looks like a bloody big fucking problem to me."

"I mean, I've got a solution. What if we don't use the old STD file at all? I've come up with a new file format that works a treat."

"But everyone uses the STD file, don't they? Isn't this what the customer is expecting?"

Tom chipped in, seeing that Dylan was struggling to articulate his vision. "The thing is, the new file format works in 3D. All we need is a converter program to get from the STD file to the new format and back again. It's a temporary fix until 2.0."

Something told me this wasn't going to be our salvation. "And how long would it take to write this converter program?"

"It's going to take a while," says Dylan. "Weeks maybe?"

"More like months surely," says Tom.

"You've all gone raving mad!" I was into full-on rant mode, storming around the War Room. "You're adding on another step that nobody wants. It's not commercial. How complicated do you want to make it? It's got to be simple. You need to go and solve the problem, not come up with a very slow temporary fix. We've missed two deadlines—another delay will finally kill us, you know that. Do you want to kill us or what?"

"No, M," said Tom, soothingly. "We don't want to kill us."

"You're killing me though!"

"Yes, but not intentionally," says Tom. "So it's more like manslaughter than actual murder, to be fair."

I didn't find this consoling thought to provide that much consolation. "We are already dead," I said, feeling like a zombie. "I would fucking fire the both of you if not for the fact that I need you too much."

There was something about my half-threatening, half-tragic, histrionic style that compelled the pair of them to work like maniacs for the next couple of weeks, to put in sleepless night after sleepless night, poring over a hot but semi-useless printer. The irony of it all was that we had millions in the bank, but we were going to have to give it all back.

And then, almost out of the blue, the miraculous breakthrough that we had all been dreaming of occurred. Dylan solved the conundrum and came up with a user-friendly file that would print color in 3D. Crisis over, bankruptcy averted, relief all round. We could make the deadline after all.

And then something else went wrong and we missed the goddamn deadline anyway.

28

THE PERFECT DAY

Give thought to a healthy work-life balance, and ensure yourself and your team have time to connect with their peers around nonwork activities. —(The Professor, "Rules for Maximum Productivity and Motivation")

It was a perfect day. "Isn't it a perfect day?" I said to Tom as I walked into the office. A lovely blue sky, a hint of warmth in the air, birds tweeting in the trees, and spring in full bloom. I had a feeling we were finally turning the corner.

He looked up from his computer. "I see that guy on the horse is looking at me again." It was true that there was one rider in particular, a regular, who had a habit as he trotted by of looking into our old farmhouse, curious about the goings-on there. Tom had taken it into his head that he was staring at him personally.

I gave him a cheerful slap on the shoulder as I went by. "Don't worry, it may never happen." I was using his favorite line for a change.

Looking back on it I can see that this unaccustomed excess of optimism on my part was bound to invite trouble. "It" happened—relentlessly, all day long. In no particular order: The Norway deal completely blew a fuse. Prices on the supply side were going through the roof. Greensboro, in North Carolina, were on the phone to Jack telling him that none of their printers worked and they wanted their money back (all half-a-million of it). "I'm not having another one!" was the oft-repeated phrase. Either there was external damage or the power packs were faulty. Jack was having a meltdown. Meanwhile, Gary was screwing us over a split delivery. Where were all the blue doors? Nothing was going right, and we were all at the end of our tether. There's a phrase Popeye comes out with, shortly before opening a can of spinach: "That's all I can stands, I can't stands no more!" We had all got to that point. Around midafternoon I said to everyone, "Time out, people! Let's forget about printers for a while. We need some foosball."

I had in mind the very sound advice of the Professor, in his "Rules for Maximum Productivity and Motivation," that we should "Give thought to a healthy work-life balance." We were stressing out so much that we were bound to make bad decisions. "You can't do a good job if your job is all you do" (*The Entrepreneur's Book of Secrets*, secret #9).

It should be understood that what I have been calling the "War Room" was, in reality, at least some of the time, more a "recreation room." Whatever you want to call it, it was a huge room, occupying the whole of the upstairs—the loft—of the farmhouse. It contained not only my desk and a long conference table but also some comfortable armchairs, a sofa, a large-screen TV, and, at the far end beneath a skylight, a foosball table (also known as "table soccer"). It wasn't always war: this is where we came to unwind and relax after all the highs and lows of the day (on this day, mainly lows). Manning a startup is, at the best of times, a stressful business, and this was definitely not the best of times. Foosball was our way of decompressing and saving our sanity.

Jack and Eden lined up against me and Dylan. For anyone who has not played the game, you aim to kick a ball in the opposition's goal by manipulating rods equipped with wooden figures. I think it was 1–1 when Jack took a call. Which upset Eden. "Don't take the call!" she yelled at him in a tone of exasperation.

"I need to take this call," says he. "From the UK."

"Well, I need this game! It's all I've got."

I really felt for her at that moment. She really made it sound as if foosball was a lifeline.

Jack wandered off downstairs. Gaston stepped in to take his place, and we carried on, but I couldn't concentrate because I could hear stray fragments of Jack's phone conversation.

"I know. . . . I told them that. . . . I completely agree."

I felt as if I was being laid neatly across the tracks and tied down, and I could already hear the train whistle in the distance.

Then finally he put the phone down and a very loud "Shit!" echoes up the stairs.

"Is everything all right?" I said, solicitously.

He marched up the stairs, gritting his teeth. "Let's just finish the game!" He wasn't in the mood for a chat.

"You're down 3–2," I pointed out.

Jack shoved Gaston out of the way.

"Come on, partner," said Eden, with the enthusiasm of a lioness who has just spotted an antelope in the distance. "Let's kill!"

"You know, technically, you're not allowed to do that, don't you?" I was, perhaps, being just a little bit pedantic. Jack was so hyper he had taken to "spinning" his rods, i.e., using his open wrist to flip his men 360 degrees at speed, thus allowing for dramatic long-distance shots at goal. One of his shots had just taken out the goal, which had come unstuck from the table.

"Fuck the rules!" says he. "That's 3-all. You just don't like to lose."

I wasn't going to get in an argument about it. He had the look of a man who was not about to split hairs over paragraph 38, subsection 2, in the rule book.

Eden and Jack shared an aggressive high five. Meanwhile Dylan was being his usual steady, unemotional self and gradually imposing himself on the game. He scored a hat trick, one goal after another, bam-bam-bam. Which didn't go down that well with Eden. "You bastard! Did you tilt the table or what?"

After that she went in harder than ever. But the table wasn't quite up to it. It was, to be honest, a slightly aging table, a little the worse for wear, which I had imported from my house. And she was giving it a battering, even apart from the screaming. One extra hard whack from her and one of her men's leg broke (note: these "foosmen" only have one central leg or two legs joined together).

"Oh that's a shame," said I, sympathetically. "Man down. We'd better stretcher him off."

"We're playing on," she said. "We are going to fucking finish this."

"I think the table has had its day."

"You'll have had your day if you don't keep playing!"

"Look," said Jack. "You can just about brush the ball with the broken leg."

Eden could scent blood. "We can do this!"

"Okay, okay," I said.

Dylan, saying nothing and remaining religiously focused on the game itself, racked up another hat trick. It was 9–3 now.

"We're not dead yet!" yelled Eden. "Comeback time. We are going in really hard now. No more Mr. Nice Guy."

That was when I scored the final goal with a deft flick into the corner. "10–3, good game," says I, diplomatically.

"You condescending sonovabitch!" Eden seemed to be not in the mood for niceties. If she'd had a boot to throw at me, she would have thrown it right then. She and Jack stormed off somewhere, muttering mutinously.

I always liked that about Eden: she was a sore loser. So am I. I'm also much more OCD than she is. Little things bug me. As soon as the opposition team had left the field, I took out my superglue and reattached both the missing leg and the vagrant goal. It wasn't perfect, but I thought Hiroshi would approve.

Foosball was supposed to be a break from the routine. But the reality was at botObjects, whether we were in the lab or the office, manning the phones or the foosball table, we were permanently on the verge of a nervous breakdown. I guess that's what the Professor means by "life-work balance." There wasn't a moment where we weren't busting a gut. And, imperfect though it may be, that's the way we got things done. If you want to make history, you might have to break a few legs. Maybe the War Room was the right name for it after all.

29

NOTOBJECTS

Nine Steps for Effective Problem-Solving

"Hey, Eden," I said, "who the fuck is this @notObjects fucker anyway?"

"It's kind of hard to say," she said. "He only has a broken 3D printer for a profile pic. They're funny tweets though!"

"Yeah, so funny I want somebody to stomp on this guy and grind him up into little pieces. He's killing us!"

"OK, boss, let me see what I can do."

Eden was the only one on my staff who called me "boss." I liked that about her. She was great at her job, quick-witted and inventive. And all the poor sad geeks in the office were in love with her. I think if they could have 3D printed their very own Eden they would have done. But that wasn't my problem. Sublimation, Freud reckons, is good for you anyway—maybe they would channel all that bubbling libido into the ProDesk 3D. My problem, in the early months of 2014, was @notObjects.

The bastard was shredding us. I suppose he thought it was all good fun originally, taking out the "bot" and making it "not." Maybe it was the revenge of one of those frustrated distributors? Or possibly a rival company trying to put the boot in? Some ancient antagonist? We had no idea. But it started bad, and it was getting worse. We were being trolled. Every time anything went wrong with our machine (which, admittedly, was only about ten times a day), @notObjects would pick up on it and broadcast it to the world. There were pictures of our most glaring mistakes and a rolling commentary on our "Greatest Wipeouts" (which I believe is surfer talk for failure). Obviously every decent tech startup is going to run into issues of one kind or another. Situation normal. But @notObjects existed to expose our hiccups and our failures and thus cause maximum embarrassment. Jack was having to work overtime to pacify and placate as worried customers called in to inquire about the latest fiasco. It began to seem like there were no secrets anymore in industry.

Naturally we assumed it was a security breach, and some bad actor was hacking into our system. So we toughened up our defenses. To begin with, Tom set up a second firewall to back up the first. But that didn't seem to make any difference. We were still getting hacked. Then I had this conversation with Tom:

WARNER: When are you going to fix this, Tom? It's getting beyond a joke.
O'BRIEN: I've been thinking about it. Here's the funny thing—I can't find any trace of an intruder.
WARNER: Maybe we need to look harder? Isn't there software that keeps track of hackers?
O'BRIEN: Yes, there is—that's what I mean. We're not picking up evidence of bad actors on the outside breaking into our computers.
WARNER: What then?
O'BRIEN: It only leaves one logical possibility.
WARNER: Which is? Come on, spit it out.
O'BRIEN: Well, it could be someone on the inside exporting data.
WARNER: What!? You mean, one of us? At botObjects?

I had failed to "think strategically," as the Professor advises. In retrospect I can see, I was utterly naive. I was relying on "team culture" and loyalty. I had no idea that one of the botObjects crew could betray the company. We were like family. We played foosball together. Of course you expect to be mugged walking down the street—but to have someone screwing you over in your own house—unthinkable! Or was it . . .?

After that it was panic stations, all hands on deck. We were under attack, inside and out. Maybe nothing we could do about skullduggery on the outside, but we could surely plug the leaks. The Professor says that there are "9 Steps for Effective Problem-Solving" (Identify the issues, discuss the high-level vision for change, etc.) In this particular case, I boiled it all down to just one—the cybersecurity specialist we called the "Terminator." His real name was Roman Jakobson (like the Russian linguist), and he was technically referred to as the "Administrator," but he always felt that wasn't quite dramatic enough so he self-identified—and ended his emails—as "The Terminator" instead. And out of respect we called him "Terminator."

Roman the Terminator's job was to police our computer system. He'd done the same job for me at P. J. Rogan and caught people trying to pocket sensitive info and had them, as he would say, terminated. He always wore Ray Ban aviators like a movie star as if he feared paparazzi or any hint of natural light. He was used to the kinds of rooms in which there are crowded banks of turbocharged processors and not much else. He worked the sort of hours in which vampires rise up and wander the earth. Roman took one look at our system, and he was like one of those contractors who gives a sharp intake of breath when he is sizing up the scale of the job in front of him. Or, perhaps more accurately, a plumber surveying how leaky the plumbing is. "It's like a sieve!" said he. "How could you be so amateurish, Bros.?" he said. "Bros." was a nickname I'd acquired at Rogan's when they got to know I was a film nut—inevitable with the name Warner (and pronounced "Broz" but commonly written, I think, as per Warner Bros., with the period to mark the abbreviation).

"We were in a hurry," I said.

"You've got zero security, Bros. A five-year old could hack into your network and play *Grand Theft Auto* with your data."

"Can you fix it?"

"Does Starbucks make coffee?"

For what he charged we could have had a Starbucks for life. But Roman set about sealing up the leaks. For starters he sent out a message to all users from "the Terminator" that their computers were being monitored and any emails containing sensitive information about the company would trip alarms. Then he actually set up the alarms, so he wasn't bluffing. No more explosive emails. No more hacking. Then he tied a knot in all the USB ports, so nobody could transfer pictures and data to a memory stick. Problem solved?

It was not long before the following hit the Twittersphere:

@notObjects: They tried to stop me telling you everything you need to know about @botObjects. But guess what—they can't. Nothing can stop the truth coming out. Suck on that dickheads.

The Terminator's precautions had so far failed to stop the whistleblower in his tracks. That was when he banned phones from campus. They were like lethal weapons, he said. From then on, phones had to be checked in at the office, picked up again on the way out. "Steve Jobs is killing us," said the Terminator. But the question remained: who, exactly, was the hit man?

Increasingly, it looked like an inside job.

30

9/11

My interview at the Twin Towers

If only Tom hadn't started calling him "bin Laden," maybe I wouldn't have had the flashbacks. "You're right," I said. "He's like a fucking terrorist! And I'm fucking paying him!"

Osama bin Laden was no more, but in the wider world, even under Obama, the so-called "war on terror" went on. But, in our very small way, we were fighting one of our own, on our doorstep. We were like Homeland Security, trying to weed out the bad guys before they could do any more damage. And if you want to know the fundamental reason I always look at planes with a degree of anxiety, it's because I was right there on 9/11, leaving my office on Wall Street and walking toward the Twin Towers.

The first time I went to Wall Street I was only seventeen, on vacation in New York with my stepdad. It was winter, and there was two feet of snow and people were skiing along Broadway. I didn't particularly want to go up the Empire State Building or visit the Metropolitan Museum; I only really wanted to go and see Wall Street, this fabled mecca of money. I looked up at the P. J. Rogan building and pointed into the sky and boldly announced to my stepdad, "One day I will have an office in that building." And thanks to my exploits in IT, my dream had come true and, a little older, I had an office in that very same building. Only now I was thinking about leaving it for pastures greener. Other banks were crying out for my system of "extreme RAD" ("rapid application development") and were willing to pay for the privilege.

If my 9 a.m. interview had been a half hour earlier, I wouldn't be creating a 3D printer company. It was exactly like a bomb going off. Not just the sound of a plane smashing into a tall building—even though I had no idea that was what it was—but the explosion of airborne material. I actually wondered, madly, if this was a mushroom cloud and I was walking right through it, but then I realized I would already be dead if it was. I was crossing Fulton Street, on the edge of Liberty Plaza, when I looked up at the Twin Towers through the sudden fog of dust and (as I later learned) asbestos. I could see the flames, and I could see people leaping into the void from a hundred stories up.

I could hear the sickening thud as they hit the ground.

So many people died that day in the financial district. Let's face it, I was one of the lucky ones. I came about as close to apocalypse as I ever want to get. We are still living with the consequences, so maybe it's not all that surprising if events at botObjects triggered flashbacks to 9/11. I kept remembering the New York cop guiding me and others uptown. "What's happening?" people were asking him. He was admirably cool and composed. I guess somebody had to be. "We don't have a full picture yet, sir. We're not exactly sure. There have been casualties. We're trying to stop adding to the list."

We got it, we kept moving—uptown. Only the emergency guys were bravely running toward the danger.

I remember the two guys fighting in the street over a T-shirt—to wrap around their faces as a mask. We were that desperate.

I remember walking ten miles uptown with fighter jets flying overhead.

I remember finally meeting my wife on the Queensboro Bridge, and we were both sobbing. We looked back downtown to where the Twin Towers had stood, and all we could see was smoke.

I remember that there were trucks going past my apartment for weeks carrying rubble.

I never did go to that interview. Maybe it wasn't meant to be. Seeing the Twin Towers be reduced to dust and rubble that day has inspired me ever since to try and create something that would go toward filling that mighty void. And now we had built something—no matter how small and fragile and precarious—and someone was trying to take us down. They couldn't be allowed to succeed.

31

GASTON

The French Connection

"Morning, Mr. Fintech!"

I had almost forgotten that old nickname—I had attained a degree of notoriety at P.J. Rogan for coming up with some industry-disrupting software and appearing on a number of front covers of magazines—with the headline "MR. FINTECH"—and thereby earning lifelong resentment and hostility from some of my more inadequate colleagues. "Morning, Terminator!"

I don't know what I expected a cybersecurity guy to do exactly: inspect people's computers, I suppose. And that is exactly what Roman did, but he went further than that: he inspected people's lives. I'm not sure he had any real reason for suspecting Gaston first of all as the source of our leaks, but he soon found reasons to report back to me. He may have worn shades all the time, but it was like he was wearing X-ray specs. No one escaped his penetrating gaze.

"You know he is in touch with people in France, don't you?" he said. Normally I had my door open on campus. When the Terminator reported to me, I had to close it.

"Well, he is French-Canadian," I said. "C'est normal!"

"Normally, I would agree with you, Bros. But you know there's a new French 3D printer company?"

"What!?"

"'Connexion3D.' You haven't heard of them?"

"Non!" I had probably reached the limit of my schoolboy French.

"You ever see *The French Connection*?"

Merde! Okay, that is the limit. Of course I knew the movie well. Gene Hackman and his porkpie hat—classic New York cop "Popeye" Doyle—on the track of the suave French drug kingpin, Alain Charnier, a.k.a. "Frog One," played by Fernando Rey. In my film buff way, I knew that Rey had also starred in the films of Luis Buñuel and he was in fact Spanish, but in my mind he was the quintessential Frenchman: always elegant, well spoken, smart, charming, and utterly devoid of morals. "You're saying that Gaston is a heroin smuggler?"

"Not exactly," said the Terminator. "He could be smuggling something more valuable than that—information."

"Fucking hell!" I blurted out. "Excuse my French."

I didn't want to be overly paranoid. But the fact is that Roman had a point. In the course of building and fine-tuning the ProDesk3D, botObjects had accumulated a bundle of trade secrets. We now had over one hundred patents. There were a lot of other competitors out there who would pay a ton of money to know what we knew, to get their hands on our tech. Even when they said, "THAT IS IMPOSSIBLE!" and accused us of being liars and crooks, you knew that, fundamentally, they feared that it was all too possible and they just didn't have the know-how that we had. What wouldn't they do to take a shortcut? What if they didn't need R&D? In other words, we were talking about intellectual theft, industrial espionage. You could hack into our system, of course, and hijack the data, but what if you had someone on the inside, wouldn't that be a whole lot easier?

Gaston, you will recall, was an open-source guy by orientation. An internet anarchist. That's how we found him. We started off downloading his firmware and then we downloaded him when we needed to adapt and adjust. That was his job—to finesse his own firmware. But the difference was, we weren't open-source. We couldn't afford to be. We had a 3D printer to sell. We couldn't just give it all away for free, could we? But what if Gaston had other ideas? He might be one of those continental radicals determined to pull the rug out from under capitalism—or, more likely, an "intrapreneur" who was running his own little side hustle selling off our secrets.

Either way I had to know. "Good work, Terminator," I said. "Do a bit more digging and let me know what you come up with." Okay, I know I was asking him to snoop on one of my trusted employees. But you couldn't take any chances. Then Roman hit me with another French word.

"Sabotage. You ever thought about it?"

"No," I said.

"Maybe you ought to."

Then he went out. Sabotage. The idea had never occurred to me. But now that he mentioned it, I had to admit that it would explain a lot. All the times we blamed the packaging for faulty machines— what if it wasn't the packaging? I had been blaming the baggage handlers in London and Tokyo, but maybe they were in reality decent, responsible citizens who protected and cared for all the fragile items in their hands. And then there were other times when the printer was working one day and then, for no obvious reason, not working the next. And it always took a lot of fixing. But what if the explanation was that someone had been going around the place unfixing it in the first place? It wasn't gremlins, it was Gaston. Or, at least, that was the thought that the Terminator had planted in my mind, and it was a hard one to shake. It explained everything that had gone wrong. Whenever I saw Gaston after that, I couldn't help wondering what he had been getting up to while my back was turned. I looked at Gaston and I started seeing Frog One.

Maybe the Terminator needed a new nickname, like Gumshoe or Sherlock or whatever—because he turned out to be genius at follow-ing clues and tracking. He was a real bloodhound. I had never taken much interest in the private lives of our employees. But he did. I guess I had just assumed that, like me, they were 100 percent focused on getting our little ProDesk3D to be the best domestic 3D printer in the world. Turns out they weren't. They actually had lives. Which included love lives.

I had no idea that Eden Burberry was some kind of femme fatale. At least that is how she was portrayed by Roman. Apparently, Gaston had fallen for her, 'ard. I suppose, now he mentioned it, Eden was a nice-looking young woman. She went jogging a lot in skimpy shorts and tank top and had a ponytail, glasses, and freckles. That was enough to drive some guys crazy. Notably Gaston. Maybe that was a peculiarly French weakness—romance, I mean. Don't get me wrong. I love my wife, and I'm all in favor of "Please Please Me," "Love Is All Around," and "Ain't No Mountain High Enough." But, let's face it, business is business. We had a 3D printer to sell, always assuming we could get it to work. I didn't think about much else. The same could not be said of Gaston.

Out of the shreds and patches of the stray emails and SMS messages he had scrutinized, gumshoe Roman managed to piece together the whole story. It had started, innocently enough, with the jogging. When she wasn't off surfing somewhere, she was a jogger; he decided he was into jogging too. So they went jogging together during lunch breaks. Why weren't they having lunch? That is yet another mystery. He said she looked "fit"; she explained to him that the word had acquired a different connotation. Yes, that too, he said. She was no doubt charmed by his Canadian/Gallic swagger. And impressed by his skill on the double bass. All that plucking. I refuse to make any double-entendre jokes about his "firmware," if only because they are already commonplace among the firmware community. In any case, it wasn't long before they were spending time together off-campus, having candlelit dinners together, sharing a bottle of French wine, before finally consummating a transatlantic liaison.

You'd think I might have noticed all this. But no, I was blissfully unaware, more concerned as I was with distributors and nozzles and flaky robots. Nor did I much notice when there was a—surely there must be a French word for this?—divergence and a cooling of passion. *Désamour*? Does that exist? At least on her side. She had already moved on. Thus leaving him high and dry and, suggested the Terminator, vulnerable to solicitation from afar—the French "Connexion3D." "One was not 'appy," as Gaston might say.

There was no actual proof of any of the above, only hints and hypotheses. Roman had no hard evidence as such. But there was yet another theory that he was keen to put in front of me. It was something that particularly intrigued him, because it was inaccessible even to his dark arts. I speak, of course, of pillow talk, the verbal exchanges that may or may not have occurred before and after physical exertions. What if Gaston was not in fact the lead in French Connection III (or whatever) and he was only what he appeared to be on the face of it, a sad French firmware virtuoso? But, nevertheless one who was apt, in moments of intimacy, to yield technical information to his *petite amie* that could be of value to our rivals and adversaries?

"Hold on!" I said. "You're saying that Eden is the bad guy in all this?"

"I'm not saying anything. But surely you want to know who was next after Gaston?"

"Who?"

32

DYLAN

You cannot be serious!

"It can't be," I said. "Gaston I understand. Like Fernando Rey—the charming villain. But Dylan—he only knows about two or three words. And he has a ring through his nose. And one ear longer than the other. He's ace at coding of course. But how does he even get to first base?"

"Exactly my point, Bros." says the Terminator. "He has no chance. The ring through the nose is like a statement to that effect. He is basically giving up. He admits that he has no interpersonal skills what-soever. So the only way anything is ever going to happen in his little world is if someone else takes the initiative. He has to be led by the nose. By the ring through his nose. By Eden Burberry."

"How do they ever get any work done?" I was shocked on that level alone. I thought of the campus as a monastery: I hadn't realized that its spirit of sacred, cloistered calm and contemplation had given way to a nonstop orgy. I was like the head monk at the lamasery in *Lost Horizon* while everyone else was auditioning for roles in *Basic Instinct* or *Fatal Attraction*.

According to Roman, it was all Eden's idea. There had been no jogging. Dylan was not that into it. No dinners at swanky restaurants; maybe a burger; certainly a latte. But there had been a lot of talk about software, he was sure of that. She said she had always been fascinated by software and she found developers irresistible and could they meet at Starbucks to discuss the intricacies of C++. They went to his place and played *Grand Theft Auto* together and *Call of Duty*. That may well have been the limit of their friendship, I don't know and I don't care. But Dylan, in between bites of burger, may well have given away the crown jewels of ProDesk3D software.

"But he's not exactly going to blab, is he?" I said. "He's constitutionally incapable of blabbing."

"Agreed," says Roman. "But he was sharing lines of code. Whole pages. Because it seemed as though she was really interested. He'd never encountered that before in a woman. She wanted to know and he was willing to tell."

"But what was she going to do with it?"

"Highest bidder," said the Terminator.

"You're saying she's the intrapreneur?"

"Give me more time and I'll crack the case wide open."

33

THE CHINA SYNDROME

Sometimes "burnout" is not a metaphor

Even while the Terminator was doing his Sherlock thing and saving us from subversion, there were more problems hitting us, this time from China. Two, to be precise: one intentional, the other, so far as I know, purely accidental.

Let's face it, China was always going to be good and bad. We went to China for many of our components, like motors and chips. But, by virtue of the same glorious monster that is globalization, they were always likely to come back at us with a printer all of their own—particularly if they could steal some of our ideas, or, to come to the point, our personnel. China was providing us with the bare necessities, but then in reverse siphoning off our top men—and women. Which is how I came to have the following conversation with Eden when she came into my office one fine day.

"Sorry I haven't come up with any answers on @notObjects, Boss."

"Don't worry about that, Eden," says I. "The Terminator's got that well in hand."

"Cool, okay, thanks. Good to know."

146 The Startup Story

I wondered if that might have a bit of an impact on our resident femme fatale, but she seemed unflustered. She was still standing there and I had a call to make to a distributor in Australia. "Was there something else?" The subtext of my question, as you will appreciate, was "Who are you fucking now and are you thereby fucking me?" I hesitated to spell it out though.

"I've had a job offer come in."

"You're in demand!"

And she was too—by Bangbang3D, based in Shanghai. They were offering her another 50 percent on top of what I was paying her. Bangbang, it was rumored, were on the verge of coming up with a new 3D printer for less than $1,000. I'd seen some illustrations online and I have to say one thing: it was so fucking *ugly*. It looked like it had been stuck together out of spare parts by a crazed hobbyist. No smooth aluminum shell. No stormtrooper's helmet. It was almost amateurish. But if they could sell it for under a thousand, it would probably find buyers. And they, or some of them, could be or should be our customers. So they were already planning to steal our customers; and now they were planning to steal our staff too. Where was it going to stop?

"Of course, I don't want to go," said Eden.

"You don't?"

"I like it here."

"Don't fancy a totalitarian pseudo-communist quasi-capitalist regime?"

She grinned. "And my Chinese is sadly lacking."

"I can offer you a raise of 25 percent. We can't afford to lose you, Eden." Should I have let her go? I was genuinely grateful to her for sticking around and scorning the approach, even if she was some kind of spy/saboteur. What's that old line, something about keeping your friends close and your enemies closer?

She looked taken aback. "Thank you, boss!"

It was actually a small price to pay for keeping the team together. I was worried that if she went then that could start a stampede—particularly if all the guys were swooning over her. So long as she stayed, they stayed, glued as they were to her jogging shorts and tank top.

Crisis averted, until the next one flared up. "Our factory just burned down," said Tom before he'd even sat down.

"What? Gary's place? Is he all right?"

"Our motherboard factory—in China."

The motherboard was the main printed circuit board in our printer—populated by the central processing unit and a bunch of chips and controllers. In other words, the brain of the whole thing. I didn't even know it was being sourced from China. "Can we find a replacement? We need to get a hundred printers out urgently." Gary was gearing up to meet the demand, but without the motherboard he could only assemble a worthless piece of junk.

"No problem," says Tom. "Lots of potential replacements. Right here in the United States. I just phoned three of them."

"That's a relief. You had me worried there for a moment."

"Soonest they can do a new order is eighteen months from now."

OMG! We were just about getting on top of the shipping problem and now this. "Fuck China and fuck the United States too," I said, trying to be evenhanded. "Surely there has to be someone somewhere in the world who can do the job! What's wrong with everyone?"

"Demand is high, supply is low."

"Oh great, so don't tell me, it's going to push the price up?"

"That's if we can get even find anyone."

"There is no 'if.' Or 'but.' What about Canada?"

Canada is usually a good backup. I love Canada: I reckon there's two weeks in the year between the point at which the snow melts and before the insects hit when it's one of the most beautiful places on the planet. Except that it turned out to be useless where motherboards are concerned. Worse even than the United States. After about a hundred phone calls, we managed to locate a small, family-run manufacturer in Reading, England, thirty miles outside London. A guy called Andy. At inordinate cost he could come up with a hundred in a fortnight. Tom flew over there and picked them up. They worked, sort of. The chips—integrated circuits—controlled the motors. But the new chips didn't work with the old motors. So all Tom had to do was strip down the old motor and reconstruct it so that it did. Times twelve. And then get in a ton of new parts for over a thousand motors. We had reinvented the 3D printer—now we were reinventing it all over again. I don't think Tom slept much for about a week or so. He was a total hero.

So it was all the more infuriating when @notObjects tweeted out, "Pssst, waiting for your @botObjects 3D printer? If I were you I'd think again—their factory in China is a pile of ashes. RIP ProDesk3D." And they had a picture of a very dead-looking incinerated factory. Almost like it had been bombed.

It was shortly after that I saw our printer online with Chinese ideograms all over it. They were clearly planning to replicate—pirate!— our printer. In China they could probably get away with walking all over our patents too. Bloody Chinese! After raging and cursing for a day or two, I decided that if you couldn't beat them you had to join them. Think about it: over one billion potential customers. Within a couple of weeks, I had signed up a Chinese distributor and, incredibly, he had already wired us half a million without any sight of the product. Which in turn created still further demand after word of the deal got around. Now all we had to do was come up with the goods.

I think it was around then that I had my vision that was right up there with a perpetual motion machine: we needed a printer that could print other printers—then all our problems would be over. Wouldn't they?

34

HELD FOR RANSOM

How to earn yourself 100 Bitcoins

The first thing I knew of the next major glitch coming over the horizon was when Eden walked in and said, "Have you seen the message on your computer?" I hadn't, because I'd been on the phone to China for the previous hour or more.

"From?"

"Have a look and you'll see."

So I took a look. I was assuming she meant some kind of email message. Not so. I couldn't even access email, but I could see the message as soon as my screen lit up. "HEY BUTTOBJECTS! SEND ME 100 BITCOINS OR YOU CAN KISS GOODBYE TO ALL YOUR DATA." It was followed by a whole string of letters and numbers that seemed to be some obscure crypto wallet address.

ButtObjects! That was so fucking rude! I wanted to reach through the computer screen and grab this guy by the scruff of the neck and give him a good shake. You might be able to guess my next semi-coherent statement and who it was addressed to. "What the fuck, Roman! What is going on around here?" You could say I was disappointed with the Terminator. I had brought him in at great expense to plug all the leaks and now this. "I don't even know how much a Bitcoin is worth!"

"It's currently around $1,000," he said. (Well, this was a few years ago. I wouldn't mind having a hundred Bitcoins now.)

I pounded the desk in front of me with my fist. "So this fucker is demanding approximately $100k! This is worse than having the Mafia on your back. It's like protection money. Pay up or else!"

"It's a sophisticated malware code an external agent has managed to insert into your system. Or 'ransomware.' They must have found some kind of back door I wasn't aware of. Or more likely one of your crew clicked on a link they shouldn't have. Sorry, Bros."

I'd never even heard of ransomware before, but you didn't need a PhD in computing science to work it out. "Can't you do something about it? You're the cyber security expert."

"I'm working on it, Bros. Give me a day."

"Fuck that! You've got an hour."

We could afford $100k, if we had to. But I didn't want to go down that road because—where was it going to stop? It was like being blackmailed, and there was nothing to stop the blackmailer coming back for another bite.

When the Terminator returned after an hour I could tell from his face that it was not good news. "The attack is based on some kind of military-level encryption. Maybe from the Israelis or the Russians. Could be the WEvil group. Maybe Yuckyuck. I can't seem to break into it."

"So what's the next step?" I was imploding, but trying to keep a lid on it.

"My guess is you're going to have to pay up unless you want your network permanently tied up in knots—sometimes it's the line of least resistance."

"Fat lot of good you turned out to be! I'm not putting good money in the pocket of a thief."

All of which will explain why I did something relatively unusual next. No, I didn't blow a fuse (not that unusual anyway); no, I didn't punch a hole in the wall or slam the terminal on the ground—even weirder than that, I decided to go for a jog. Well, not exactly jogging, more a fast-paced walk, driven by anger and frustration. Since the system was down I had nothing better to do. Talk about sea of troubles. I'm not saying it was the last straw, but it felt like maybe the penultimate straw. I would have checked myself in at the NYU hospital again, but it was too far away. You have to remember our campus was way out in the country.

I needed to get away from it all for half an hour. Blow off some steam, clear my head, see if I could come up with any fresh ideas. There had to be a way out, surely? I just couldn't figure out what. After all, I had been something of a software aficionado myself back in the day, but I'd outsourced all the heavy lifting. And I wasn't hacker level, that was for sure. If the Terminator couldn't break the code, there was no way I could. Even though I wasn't really in the mood for it, I had to admit it was a beautiful spring day, warm enough to go wandering through the fields in just a light jacket. I followed a path into the woods and felt hot enough to enjoy a bit of shade. Birds were singing in the trees. I crossed a wooden bridge across a bubbling brook when I caught sight of someone else out for a jog. Eden Burberry. She was running toward me, perhaps on her way back to campus. She wasn't alone either: there was another blonde, ponytailed woman running alongside her, also wearing Edenesque shorts and tank top. It was like seeing double. I assumed she was another surfer girl.

"Hey, Eden!" I called out. So far as I knew she was the source of a lot of my woes, but at least she wasn't holding the company for ransom. She was technically competent, obviously, but she wasn't hacker level either.

"Hey, boss," she called back, waving.

The two of them ran right up to me and stopped. After some expression of amazement on both sides that we were meeting like this, Eden said, "My girlfriend, Tiffany, this is my boss, Martin Warner."

"Pleased to meet you, Tiffany," says I.

Tiffany nodded politely. "I've heard so much about you," she said, with a grin. I could see now, at close quarters, that she wasn't exactly a clone of Eden: she was slightly taller, darker, more muscular. Her tank top had the words, "USC ATHLETICS," printed across it. Maybe athlete more than surfer, but fit-looking either way.

They ran off again, and I walked on, mulling over our brief exchange. Well, of course, Tiffany was a girl and a friend, so therefore a girl friend. But the way she said it: why would she even bother unless it was more than just a girl-space-friend? I turned around and hurried back to campus, almost seriously justifying the verb "to jog."

I sat down in the office and rather than ask to speak to her, I texted Eden.

WARNER: Good to meet your friend, Tiffany.
BURBERRY: She was impressed to see you out enjoying the countryside.
WARNER: You said she was your "girlfriend?"
BURBERRY: She's lovely, isn't she? Yes, we are a couple.
WARNER: Great!

I was about to text her, "So you're not bisexual, are you, by any chance?" But I thought that would be pushing it too far, boss or not. I may be "autistic" as my mother used to say, but even I could work out from the way she spoke and smiled when she was with Tiffany that she was just not that into guys.

WARNER: Did Roman the Terminator ever hassle you about anything?
BURBERRY: No, not really.
WARNER: But did he [I struggled for the right phraseology around here] make any propositions?
BURBERRY: He asked me out once. I told him I would love to but I had a very jealous girlfriend ha ha.

Obviously I needed to have a word with the Terminator. But he had gone back to New York, ostensibly to consult with his fellow cybersecurity dudes in case they could figure out a solution to our little problem. So I texted him instead.

BROS.: You know when you called me "Mr Fintech?"
TERMINATOR: Term of respect.
BROS.: You were remembering one of those magazine headlines, right?
TERMINATOR: Back of my mind.
BROS.: Funny how so many people at Rogan's hated me for that.
TERMINATOR: Jealous fools!
BROS.: And now you're trying to gouge me for 100 Bitcoins?
TERMINATOR: What?!
BROS.: Eden Burberry is lesbian. No way is she fucking Gaston and Dylan.
TERMINATOR: Bros., you can't trust her. She is taking you to the cleaners.
BROS.: I'm going to take you to the fucking cleaners. And you will never work in cybersecurity again. Unless you get this network up and running in five minutes.
TERMINATOR: [pause] I'll do my best.
BROS.: Yeah, you do that.

Well, I wasn't going to say thanks.

My computer was fully functioning five minutes later. I didn't have to pay anyone 100 Bitcoins. And @notObjects ceased to tweet.

I have to admit: that was about the stupidest thing I did in the whole mad existence of botObjects. I had invited in a Trojan horse. But the Terminator had been—at long last—terminated.

That close encounter with an antagonist was a painful waste of time and resources, but at least I was able to realize one small thing: that, fundamentally, botObjects was all about truth. We wanted to make objects that were as true to the original concept as was technologically possible—we were the high fidelity of 3D printing. And, more than that, we hated all the liars and the fakers and the frauds, the guys who were only in it for the money. The thieves.

35

THE TWENTY-DOLLAR BILL

The Professor says, "Take as long as possible to make smart and focused decisions and reflect coolly on all your options."

It was, you will say, only twenty dollars. But twenty dollars is twenty dollars. I don't care how well-off you are, twenty dollars is not to be sniffed at. On the other hand, is it worth getting your throat cut for?

We were standing outside Grand Central Terminal, my wife and I. She had insisted on a weekend away from botObjects and all the usual *Sturm und Drang*. We had a couple of suitcases with us, and I guess we must have looked like naive tourists, fresh in from the sticks. Suckers, in other words. Which is exactly how I behaved, lulled into a false sense of security by a couple of days of bracing walks along the beach.

We went over to the first cab in line. "Charles Street," says I, leaning in.

"Hop in."

So far so normal. But it was at this point that a tall, young guy dressed in some kind of overcoat intervened. He was barely old enough to have stubble on his chin. "That'll be twenty dollars, sir."

I thought it was something like at the airport where you often have to pay up front. I was already easing a twenty-dollar bill out of my wallet at the same time as I was saying, "But don't you normally pay on arrival?"

While I was thus pondering and wondering, the kid snatched the twenty-dollar bill out of my hand and ran off down the street at top speed. It was a classic scam. It might even be a decent earner. Twenty dollars for—what?—one minute's work? If he could keep that up I reckon he'd be earning more than me.

But just at that particular moment I didn't feel like this was a legitimate form of employment. The fact is I had been ripped off. But I didn't want to be ripped off. I wanted to get my twenty dollars back. So I took off after him. Stupid, I know. But I was younger and stupider then, and, to be fair, twenty dollars was worth more back in the day. I was fitter too. So, fast though the thief was, I reckon I was faster. Also he stopped running at a certain point, confident that I was bound to let it go. But I didn't let it go. I wanted my twenty dollars back.

"OK, you worthless little scumbag," I huffed, furiously, grabbing him by the collar, while sucking in some oxygen and resisting the urge to bend over and put my hands on my knees. "Give me back my twenty dollars." It occurred to me that his pseudo-official looking overcoat had probably slowed him down, and it made it easier to get a grip on him.

"Oh man," says he, recovering from his initial bemusement, "I don't have your twenty. The cabdriver has it." There was a tone of, If I had it, I would for sure give it to you, but alas it's gone.

"I saw you take it."

"I passed it to the driver. He's got it, believe me."

I didn't believe him of course. The sincerity was just a front. But when I considered the possibility of rooting through this guy's pockets in search of the twenty, it occurred to me—for the first time—to wonder what else he might be carrying in his pockets other than my twenty. Drugs, of course. Coke, crystal meth, heroin? All of the above. But wasn't it likely that he possessed a knife or a gun too? This was

New York, after all. It wasn't quite the *Death Wish* era, where you hardly dared take the subway, but it was still a concrete jungle.

It was around this same time that I started to question my sanity in running after the guy in the first place. Was it really worth putting myself in the way of harm, perhaps death, for the sake of a twenty? The risk–reward ratio didn't seem to justify it. Then again, I had left my wife and our belongings entirely exposed and unprotected on the street outside Grand Central. Ripe for the taking of. What was I thinking? But it was too late to back out now.

"Ok, fuckface, let's go and find out which one of you has the twenty." I wrapped my arm around his arm and marched him forcefully back to the taxi stand. The cab was still there. As was my wife, who was looking on with horror as I manhandled this poor little American Oliver Twist, no doubt betrayed by the system, driven to thievery against his better judgment.

"Which one of you assholes has my twenty?" I barked at the pair of them. As I leaned down to get my message across to the driver, so the real thief took his chance and ran off for the second time. I gazed after my fast-receding twenty, but, after careful consideration, decided to let it go.

Part of the consideration was my wife protesting, "Are you completely mad? You dump me and our cases for the sake of a few dollars?"

I was about to say, "Well, it was a twenty!" But I thought better of it and bit my tongue. I guess I wasn't really expecting any congratulations for my short-lived heroism. We finally got in the taxi, and my wife paid the fare with a twenty. "I don't want you flipping your lid all over again," says she as we got out.

She was speaking like the Professor on this occasion: "Implementing and Measuring Effective Financial & Operational Metrics for Decision Making: take as long as possible to make smart and focused decisions and reflect coolly on all your options." As I lay awake in bed that night revisiting this archetypal scene of poor decision-making, I conceded that she had a point. But sometimes you have to act and react on the spur of the moment. You don't always have time to make up a spreadsheet. On this occasion, I achieved absolutely nothing. But the underlying reality was I needed that twenty. I had worked hard for that twenty. I would willingly donate that twenty to a good cause, maybe on occasion to a guy in bad shape on the street or in the subway. But even if bot-Objects had a few million in the bank, it was always hanging by a thread, and I knew that I could end up in worse debt than the lanky kid who stole my twenty. The other difference between us is that I would never knowingly rip off anybody. I wanted to make sure that all our customers got their money's worth. And the ProDesk3D cost a lot more than twenty. They believed in us, and I wasn't about to let anyone down, much less run away with anyone's hard-earned cash. Delivery was imminent. It was a question of integrity (see The Entrepreneur's Book of Secrets, secret #39).

Overall, though, you would have to say, if somebody is tough and rough enough to steal a twenty note, you should probably let it go. And the fact is, I learned from my experience. A few years after this episode, while I was writing this book, I was walking down the street in London, rashly looking at my phone, and a guy wearing a mask drove past me on his e-scooter. Then he doubled back and stopped me. "Give me your watch and your wallet!" he said.

I looked him in the eye. "Fuck you, asshole!" was the first phrase that entered my head. But I decided to let it go this time around. Sometimes doing nothing is your best option. "No problem," I said. I took off my watch and took out my wallet and handed them over. The watch was insured, and all I had to do was cancel the cards. Maybe there was a twenty-pound note in the wallet. I had learned my lesson. Let it go. Be cool. Feel free to drive away with my worldly goods, dude, but you will not take my entrepreneurial soul. As the Professor wisely points out, "Risk is reality . . . but the level of risk can be reduced/managed if you evaluate these risks and steer toward the best possible outcome."

The fact that the guy on the scooter was also waving a knife the size of a machete—or possibly that Japanese sword in Kill Bill—in my

face and jabbing it rather convincingly toward my left eyeball probably helped steer my decision-making in this case.

Another lesson learned: Don't walk down the street sporting a
Rolex GMT Master (known to aficionados as "Root Beer" for its
two-tone bezel) on your wrist, not even in Mayfair. This is where 3D
printing comes into its own: print yourself a Rolex, and you won't
mind too much letting it go. But can you print a twenty-dollar note?
We had just the man to answer that question—Robert Storm.

36

ROBERT STORM

You can email him at robert.storm@botObjects.com

There is an issue that all startups face at a certain point: they just don't have enough people to go around. They are too small and they need to grow. Which, to an extent, we did. We were a grand total of fifteen people at our maximum. But still that wasn't enough. So we did what all small companies do in these circumstances: we expanded, virtually, notionally, in terms not of any physical staff but in departments and spheres of specialization. We may have only been small, but we had R&D of course (Tom/Gaston/Dylan), customer services (Jack), sales (Eden), communications (Eden), HR (me/Tom), legal and corporate (Patrick), finance, strategy, security and so on. The organizational structure grew, adapted, and adopted, as and when. For example, sometimes it was as simple as someone phoning up and saying, "Can I speak to your tools and accessories department, please?" "Sure, can you just hold for a moment? . . . Do we have a tools and accessories department?" "We do now—Jack, you're it." We each had to wear multiple hats.

Robert Storm was head of confirmations. I mean, someone had to be. And if you're wondering what the hell the "confirmations department" was supposed to be doing, wonder no more: it was everything that we couldn't figure out what to put under any other heading. Its most urgent priority was the category of things that cannot be categorized. I think it started with Brazil and the offer that was too good to be true. I still have regrets about that. Wouldn't you, about turning away good money? Even if it's bad.

As you will now be aware, we made an awful lot of money, millions, before we sold a single unit of our printers. All perfectly legal and straightforward: these were, in effect, "preorders" or deposits on future acquisitions. Above all, the income came from distributors, so when we heard from a distributor in Rio that they wanted to buy one thousand of our printers, we couldn't have been more excited. But ultimately we had to fall back on confirmations, and the nonpareil negotiating skills of Robert Storm.

It wasn't so much that we couldn't come up with one thousand printers. Not at all. Needless to say, we couldn't come up with one thousand printers, nowhere near, but we had by now learned the art of stringing customers along for long enough to, in the course of time, fulfill their order. The course of time in question being a rather long one, but, with persistence and our usual spirit of know-how and can-do, we would get there in the end. It might be that many of them would not in fact work, but these things could be fixed—didn't our old friend Hiroshi maintain that it was better that way, anyhow, to be flawed and fallible and in need of repair? Satisfaction guaranteed—so long as you had the patience of Job. Delivery was not an issue: our anxiety was that we were being paid too much money.

I'm not sure this is something the Professor really understands. He is all about what he calls "credit accretion," "maximizing," "accumulating," "escalating," in other words, forever upping the profit side of the equation. As gangster Edward G. Robinson, or "Johnny Rocco," says in *Key Largo* when asked by Humphrey Bogart what he wants: "I want more, yeah, MORE!" Not that I am drawing a direct analogy between the Professor and a gangster. But sometimes perfectly legitimate commercial enterprises share certain common denominators with the criminal underworld. We're all doing business (it's just theirs happens to be on the wrong side of the law). On the other hand, you have to draw the line somewhere. We had a cap on distributor deposits of half a million. That was enough to get you priority treatment. Brazil was offering us two million, four times our limit. We suggested floating up toward 750k; they counter-proposed one million, and they weren't prepared to offer any less. Our haggling them down rather than up sounds on the face of it counterintuitive. Why not take the money and . . . not run exactly, but just square it away in the bank for a rainy day?

There is one simple answer to this: money laundering. We were not allowed to touch ill-gotten gains. We were obliged, according to the strictures of the SEC (Securities and Exchange Commission), to be on the alert for money launderers. Two million was a red flag. One million would probably set off alarm bells in the higher echelons, and we would see investigators in dark glasses swooping on our humble campus. On the other hand, we didn't want to piss anyone off and lose a customer.

Which is where our hero Robert Storm comes in. "You need Robert Storm in confirmations."

"We do?"

"Oh yes, he will deal with it."

"When can we expect an answer?"

"I'll get Robert to come back to you right away."

"Can I talk to him now?"

"I'm afraid not, Robert prefers to communicate via email only."

"Really?"

"He even has a slogan: 'The best time to call me is to EMAIL me.'" (Lifted from *The Entrepreneur's Book of Secrets*, secret #29).

Whenever a situation looked as if it was beyond our powers to deal with, we called in Robert Storm. Whenever Jack couldn't take the flak any more, we naturally turned to Robert Storm. Whenever Eden finally ran out of sound bites, Robert Storm came to the rescue. He was our extra man on the boundary. He was our wingman. He was our enforcer. The other thing about him you should know is that he didn't exist. It was Eden who came up with the name in the first place. Perhaps he was her dream guy (not, of course, that she was that into guys): tough yet tender. Tall, dark, and ruggedly good-looking no doubt. But since we had no one who fitted that description, she herself had to be Robert Storm. If she couldn't handle it anymore, anyone of us could step in and take the mantle of Robert Storm. As a desperate last resort, I have stood in for Robert Storm. He is like one of those Hollywood action heroes that are too expensive to risk in a fight scene, so you draft in doubles and stuntmen. And all you need, as originally set up by Eden, is an email account in his name: robert.storm@botObjects.com.

Our Brazilian contact was a woman named Carmen. She represented an organization that she called "Lobo" that didn't seem to have any online existence. I'm not saying they were necessarily criminal, or that they were money-laundering, and least of all that they were involved in drug smuggling, but she did ask some strange questions. "Can you print new credit cards?" was one of them. "Can it print actual money?"

"I don't think so."

"What volume is the ProDesk3D?"

Eden could easily field that question: "96,446 cubic centimeters—it's much more compact than the average." The fact was that the volume tended to go up and down like a yo-yo, depending on whether Gary had managed to cram everything in or not.

"What is the volume of space that is not occupied by hardware?"

"Erm . . . Robert Storm will get back to you."

We did try and measure the available space, but we couldn't help wondering: What are Lobo planning to do with it? Did they want to pack something else in there? A substance of some kind? It was a problem for Robert Storm, without a doubt.

Sometimes Robert Storm had all the fun. There was that occasion when we were contacted by a beautiful young woman named Suzi. We called her "the Girl from Ipanema." She was wearing a skimpy bikini, and she had a lovely all-over tan. I know this because she sent us her photograph, via email. She invited Jack down to Lima (not Ipanema, I know, but it's close and it rhymes) where she would meet him in a hotel. Jack, for once, seemed to be enjoying his job. She assured him that she had a particular weakness for guys in customer service and looked forward to his attention. He still occasionally wonders what might have happened had I not deputed Robert Storm to go in his place. "But what if she's real?" he moaned.

Of course, not everyone appreciated the endeavors of our colleague Mr. Storm. He would reply only intermittently. There were long periods of silence. He almost certainly lost us business with more than one Russian oligarch. And when it came to those face-to-face encounters, he was like Macavity the Mystery Cat—he's not there! Our Brazilian friends in particular became frustrated and then angry with his lack of application. "He will email you right back." "But I can't seem to reach him!" Finally, I had to intervene: I apologized profusely for my colleague, or rather ex-colleague. "We had to let him go. He just wasn't up to the job." I must have sacked him five or six times, he was so poor.

With or without Robert Storm, we "confirmed" a lot of deals. And then there came a time when there was no point striking a new deal.

37

EITHER/OR

One eye on the build, one eye on the exit

It was one Sunday in the spring of 2014—I was exhausted from doing the round of venture capitalists—that I picked up the message from Mimetics3D. The first approach. I had been half-expecting it.

Remember that Mimetics3D were then the biggest 3D printer company in the world, with the longest history and the top-selling range of machines. So it was a little like getting a message from Arnie Schwarzenegger if you're a bodybuilder, or let's say from Steve Jobs if you happen to be making computers or phones.

Except it didn't quite come right from the top. Molly O'Hagan, in their mergers and acquisitions department, suggested that we might like to consider "teaming up" with 3D, "collaborating" and "sharing." We could enter into a "partnership" or "joint venture" (Cf. The Professor: "Joint venture/Partnership—generally involving two firms sharing resources and strengths to create a joint revenue stream. A joint venture typically involves the creation of a joint entity structure"). It seemed like a good idea at first glance. The reason being we were just starting to realize that this was a bigger job than we had ever conceived. Maybe we had bitten off more than we could chew.

I couldn't help thinking, it was a helluva big fat coincidence that they got in touch right after we got rid of the Terminator. But then again, maybe that's all it was.

We were manufacturing printers, and we were making money. Everything was going according to plan. So, you might say to yourself, what could possibly go wrong? Well, the fact is we needed to do more testing and make more improvements—the printer was still a work in progress. There were only three things that needed fixing or finessing: the hardware (the anatomy of the printer); the firmware (the brain); and the software (which would speak to the customer). In other words, everything.

But more important than that, we needed to scale up. The question was: How did we get production up to 50,000 or 100,000 units? If we were to splash out on some aggressive advertising we would hit those kind of sales figures easily. One simple answer to the problem was: inject another $10 million or so. Gary's factory was good for producing a thousand units tops. If he was going to multiply that by a factor of fifty or one hundred, then we would have to build a whole new factory, the giga factory of his dreams.

I felt that being in charge of the botObjects operation was a bit like being Charlton Heston in *Ben-Hur*. I was whipping the horses to go faster and they were going faster, but there is likely to come a moment where you make mistakes in prototyping or fabrication— and the wheels fall off. And that's without worrying about what the competition are getting up to.

Looking into the future, it was clear that we were going to have to go big to make a real dent in this market. We had to expand or shrink, curl up, and die. The pressure was that everyone would think we were failures. We had announced our entrance with plenty of fan-fare, only then to crawl offstage with our tails between our legs? It was unthinkable. We needed to deliver on our potential. Looking into my crystal ball, I reckoned we could be a $250 million company in a year or two, then heading up toward $1.6. or 1.7 billion, assuming development was linear, all the way up into the stratosphere. We still assumed that every smart home was going to need one of our printers. The Mimetics3D top man, Riley Griffin, was giving Ted talks saying exactly that. It's not as if we were alone in our vision. They had even appointed the music entrepreneur and front man of the Black-Eyed Peas, will.i.am, as their brand ambassador (or "chief creative officer") and he was going about telling everyone how much they needed a 3D printer. And for all I knew writing songs about it too.

So the only way was up and for that we would have to seek out further investment. And that's exactly what I did. I was an old hand in the realm of venture capital. Without too much effort I conjured up a preliminary pool of $15.5 million. The trouble was we were of necessity slowly diluting our share and control of the company. We were about to lose around 20 percent of botObjects. It felt a little bit like chopping off an arm or a leg.

In my previous life I had been a specialist in mergers and acquisitions. I was virtually an M&A virtuoso. But we were faced with some major strategic choices, so I went to put it all in front of Tom in the War Room. "This shit's just got real!" I said, lighting a calming cigar and trying to stop pacing up and down. I spelled out the options.

Tom poured himself a mug of black coffee. "The question is, do we need them or do they need us?"

"They need us!" I said, puffing forth a cloud of sublimely confident smoke. "We have the patents on full color—they're stuffed without that."

"There's nothing to stop us going to have a chat with them, is there?"

"There is one thing that occurs to me."

"What's that?"

"We don't have a fucking printer that works."

Tom paused to consider this vital point. "Does that matter?"

"I think they're going to want to do more than just sit around, drink coffee, and chat. We are going to have to show them the color of our money. We need another demo. Can we do that?"

"Well . . ."

"That's a no, then."

So in the end I put further financing on hold—we didn't want to lop off a chunk of the company, not yet anyway.

And I turned down Molly O'Hagan. "Thanks but no thanks" was my message. We couldn't afford the "distraction" at this time, I told her. It was too early to think about fraternizing. For one very simple but significant reason: We couldn't afford to let them see the ProDesk3D printer in action—or possibly inaction. We needed to be optimistic in our line of business, but also realistic. Our baby was brilliant, beautiful, unique—but also flaky. We had to make sure it worked reliably before showing it off to the world leader in 3D printers. It could have been embarrassing. There were still bugs. There were still packaging problems. There was still work to be done (hardware, software, firmware—that's all).

Or, to put it in a more positive way, we made the conscious decision to focus on growing the business. That had to be the number one priority. We hadn't gone far enough yet.

But my slogan remained: one eye on the build, one eye on the exit.

38

WE HAVE LIFTOFF!

Sometimes you need to draw a veil

We were finally on top of everything. Our little printer was everything we had dreamed it would be. Technically speaking, we had dotted every last i and crossed every t. I notice that lawyers, when they
have closed a case, bundle all the documents together and tie a pink
ribbon around it. This was our pink ribbon day. All those engineering
problems? A thing of the past. What about software? Ha! Sorted. And
don't even ask about firmware: the firmware was firm, as it should
be. Our firewalls were fully restored. We were rock solid, unimpeach-
able, flawless. We had loosened up one or two deadlines. No one was
screaming at me down the phone. Calm had followed the storm.

Which is why we went to the London 3D Print Show at Earls
Court with a spring in our step and a song in our hearts. Our troubles
were over. Weren't they?

The show was huge, and all our competitors were there: Mimetics3D,
Stratasys, MakerBot. And all the bloggers and industry journos. It was
almost like an old school reunion. The fact was that we were getting
all the attention. We had the longest queues. We were emblazoning

all our publicity with phrases like "the most beautiful 3D printer in the world" or "the most innovative 3D printer in the world"—and the weird thing was that people seemed to agree. Except, of course, for our immediate rivals. They were just flat-out annoyed with us for using "the most anything" tag. And for pulling in more punters than anyone else. We were really motoring now. Everything was on track. We had forty or fifty enthusiasts crowding round the latest iteration of the ProDesk3D and salivating over it like it was a Lamborghini Diablo or a Porsche Spyder. We were not only ahead of the field, but it felt like we had crossed the line and could afford to have a bit of a breather before someone came along and hung a gold medal around our necks.

And then the plastic started lifting off.

I can't even remember what we were making at the time. But it was starting to come up from the base. No one else could see it—not yet anyway—but we could. We could virtually feel it and smell it. The printer was perfect, it should be said, when it was perfect. But everything had to be equally perfect and there was a lot that could potentially go awry. In particular the platform had to go down while the ink had to go up. The net effect was that there was a propensity for the base to be drawn upward, whereas what you wanted of a base was that it should stay put and provide a solid foundation for the rest of the object. The printer was designed to flex from side to side, but not up/down. It was fundamental that the base had to stay down while the rest of the object was gradually built up, layer by layer.

Despite which, the base was popping up like an inappropriate erection. And we had to find a way to cover it up, even though we were completely surrounded by gawpers. It was like one of those classic nightmares in which you're walking down main street completely naked. Aaaaaargh!

We were desperately in need of a fig leaf.

We could have tried to pretend that everything was normal and that we had always planned to take a walk in the park with no clothes on. "Oh it's actually a little flying saucer and we wanted it to take off like that." As it was we looked at one another and Tom said, "We're

closing for lunch now. We'll be back for questions in twenty minutes."
It was like the end of Part I. It had always been scheduled that way.
Part II later. Thank you and goodbye.

We literally drew a veil over the printer—a little curtain that we
had rigged up for circumstances, much like these, that might occur.
It never does any harm to be prepared, especially where 3D printing is concerned. But people were hanging about and still asking us
questions, and we needed to get rid of them—because we needed
to dump the object-that-was-not-an-object. So long as it sat there it
was an all-too-visible stain on our escutcheon. Bloggers were going
to pounce on it as proof that botObjects was a big fat scam after all.
Beautiful box 'n' all, okay, but did it work? No!

I did my best to lure people away from the machine while talking
to them and telling them how wonderful it was. When they had their
backs turned, Tom stuck a hand down into the oven and yanked out
the evil blob that threatened to pull the rug out. He scraped the platform clean so that we could start again. We always would start again
with the ProDesk3D. We never lost faith, but even the most committed of 3D fans would have to admit: it might be the sexiest printer out
there, but it was also for sure the highest maintenance. It probably was
the most beautiful, the fastest, etc. But the reality was that we wanted
it to be better. We wanted it to go faster, with better resolution—and
no unintended liftoff.

Tom pulled it out of his pocket later that day—the blob. "What
was it supposed to be anyway?" I said.

"A unicorn," said Tom. "Multicolor, of course."

I looked at it. I didn't want to touch it as such. It reminded me
of a horror story by Ray Bradbury in which someone has all their
bones removed and collapses into a heap. Described, memorably, as a
"puddle."

"We've still got a way to go," I said.

39

ADDICTION

Take good care of our baby.

The nurse told me to count down from ten. I think I got to seven, then everything turned black and I was gone.

I was going to write that this all happened to a good friend of mine called Fred or Bob, cursed with an addictive personality. But my instinctive honesty has won out over discretion. The addict was me. I was a smoker. So as soon as I got these terrific pains in my chest and found myself writhing around the floor in agony, I naturally assumed that this had to be cancer induced by years of smoking the biggest, fattest, most fragrant (and carcinogenic?) cigars I could lay my hands on. I was getting my just desserts, finally. I was working right through it but I automatically assumed I was a goner, for all practical purposes. Maybe we could finally get the printer working properly and delivered intact to customers before I conked out. Or maybe I would never get to see that greatly anticipated miracle take place.

I was taken to hospital for the tests. They had to knock me out, because they were planning to have a good poke around in there and leave no stone unturned. I had a room the size of a cell, and I went in there thinking I would likely never come out. They would discover a tumor the size of Havana, and it would be curtains. Game over. I didn't like to tell Tom, but I left him instructions in an envelope to be opened only in the event of my not coming back. I think the letter might have been stained with a few tears: I was leaving everything unfinished; my whole crew left in the lurch; the ProDesk3D still only a contender rather than fully realizing the all-conquering destiny we had anticipated. I wanted to pour my heart out, and go on about how I'd left everything undone, but what I said was: Tom, you can do this. You don't need me anymore. We created the ProDesk3D, and now we've created the organization to produce printers at scale. Over to you, mate. I racked my brains to end on a positive note. And then a snatch of an old song floated into my head. "Take good care of our baby," I wrote. botObjects would live on without me, I thought, or rather hoped. Underneath it all I had doubts. Was this the end for me and the company?

I cursed myself for smoking that cigar in the Jacuzzi and all the other cigars I had burned through over the decades. Images of times my cigar club had filled an entire jet with smoke floated back to me. I smoked in boardrooms, bedrooms, and bathrooms. How could I have been that deluded? As I sat in the chair supervised by the nurse with the needle, the last thing that passed through my mind before the lights went out was: the vision of the pink whistle and then teasing a note out of it, and how that was like the start of the game and now I wouldn't be able to see it through to the end and . . . darkness descends.

Having a general anesthetic is not like falling asleep: there is no dreaming, all sense of time passing vanishes too. It's more like a rehearsal for the big sleep. So it was that I woke up what seemed like the next second but was in fact several hours later. A great hunk of time had just been carved right out of my life, and I'd never get it back. On the other hand, it was probably the first straight run of more than three hours together where I hadn't been thinking or dreaming or worrying about 3D printers ever since Tom knocked on my door over a year before with the pink whistle in his hand.

"What's the verdict, doc?" I said, after I'd gathered my senses and I saw the man in a white coat standing in front of me, and what looked like clinical notes on a clipboard in his hand. "Give it to me straight." I was expecting the worst—three months, six months? What would I do if that was all the time I had left? What would become of botObjects?

"You want the good news first?"

"If there is any."

"No sign of cancer."

I could hardly believe it. "Are you sure?"

"Not a shadow. Not a shadow of a shadow."

I let out a huge sigh. Doom averted. For now.

"But you have a stomach ulcer. Probably stress-induced. We're going to treat it with powerful antibiotics."

The ulcer remained uncomfortable for a couple of weeks, and I lost my appetite, but the treatment worked. I felt a bit like whoever it was, when asked what inspired him to get down to work in the morning, replied, "I read the obituaries and if my name is not there, then I carry on." Martin Warner would not be found in obits, not for a while at least, so I just got back to where I left off. One thing I realized: Had I been given only three months to live, I would have been just the same. I couldn't leave botObjects and the whole botObjects crew high and dry, dangling over the abyss. It was too soon for us to part company. I would have been striving with all the short span of life left to me to finally steer the ship out of dock and get it sailing on the high seas.

I tore up the letter I had written to Tom. botObjects and I weren't ready to go our separate ways just yet. They needed me as much as I needed them. Amazon without Jeff Bezos? Tesla without Elon Musk? Virgin without Richard Branson? Perhaps, in the end, they could keep semiautonomously rolling independent of their original driver. But not for a good long while.

That brush with cancer had the positive spin-off of stopping me smoking (eventually, after I'd recovered from the shock of nearly getting cancer). But it also helped me understand one other thing. I wasn't really addicted to nicotine or cigars. I'd known two guys who became addicted to alcohol. When the doctors told them it was time to quit they couldn't do it. Even if it was going to cost them their lives. And it did. I was addicted just as much to business, to the life of the entrepreneur, in all its agony and ecstasy, and to performing life-saving surgery on a certain dysfunctional 3D printer. I wasn't driven by the lure of profit: only by the fear of death and the compulsion to get as much as humanly possible done before the brief candle sputters and goes out.

40

YOU'RE TELLING ME

Make sure staff feel connected to their own development and their role in the overall goal and business. (One of the Professor's "13 Personal Habits")

The sad thing about this is that he was my best friend, at the time. Certainly one of the oldest. I first met Minnesota Milt at P. J. Rogan's. I remember he impressed the hell out of me with one of his flow diagrams. Milton and I were on the same floor and we shared a water-cooler. We used to talk about financial instruments and how to speed them up. He was one of the smartest guys I knew, with more letters after his name than the alphabet. And yet he was also one of the stupidest.

Well, then, why did you make him operations manager? The answer to that is simple: he was efficient, he was competent. When we were setting up botObjects, he was the first guy I thought of who was capable of overseeing and keeping a grip on just about everything: finance, production, delivery, customer service, reporting, the whole shooting match. He was the one who provided data oversight on distributors. And yet . . .

I'll give you an example of what I mean. We were once playing table tennis together (or Ping-Pong, if you will), Milt and I. Admittedly we were playing in a garage at the time, and maybe it was a hot kind of a day and maybe he was playing out of his skin. But still it came as a bit of a surprise when he put his bat down and stripped off, right down to his briefs, and then continued playing as if this was all perfectly normal. I put it down to his will to win, which was right up there with my own. But in any case it enables me to report that he had the hairiest back of any guy I've known, and chest too. A regular bear rug. Or, I suppose, bear, pre-rug.

Despite which, we became best buddies, to my way of thinking. We were like brothers, and I became godfather to his kids. I'd known him for more than a decade when I asked him to come and work for me, and even though he was taking a pay cut, he did. He was then in his late thirties and that all-over hair of his was turning gray. He rented a house near the campus and was often the first man in of a morning.

He was never going to make the grade as our roving international ambassador. He could be a bit of a robot, to be honest. Or one of those old mainframes that take an age to light up and respond to commands. Here is what I mean. I might say to him, "Milt, I would like you to go to Bahrain, in two weeks' time, and deliver fifty printers." He would look at me, the wheels would spin around, then he would reply, "You're telling me that you want me to deliver fifty printers, in two weeks' time, to Bahrain?" Or again, "Milt, can you take over this motherboard project in Seattle in September?" "You're telling me you want me to go to Seattle, in September, and take over the motherboard project?" This crazy habit of his could sometimes get to me, on a bad day. "Of course that's what I'm fucking telling you!" I might yell back at him. "You're just shuffling my words around like some kind of mad machine, why do you do that?" You'd think he might kick it, but he never did.

As I say, he was a genius with a spreadsheet or a graph, but he never really cracked social interaction. Nevertheless, he did get married to a Latvian woman. I don't know how she put up with him. "You're telling me you would like me to pass you the salt?" "You're telling me you want me to pick up some spaghetti from the supermarket on my way home?" It had to be grounds for divorce.

There was another time when we were on a business trip to Antigua, something to do with KPMG. I said to him, "Milt, don't say anything, okay, unless you have anything sharp and witty to say, leave it to me." So of course he replies, "You're telling me you don't want me to say anything on this trip." Despite which, he did. And it was neither sharp nor witty. So I'm back in New York and I get a call from one of the party. "Who is that guy Milt? Does he have a screw loose or what?" I had to explain that he really didn't, but he could sometimes give that impression.

You'd have to say he was doing a top job keeping the wheels on at botObjects. He was a rock. You could always rely on him. Or so I thought. Then there was the Mexico fiasco. And it was all Milt's fault.

We were chugging along. We had 20 million in the bank. Milt said, "We will need a further 6,679 units by year's end to meet the demand." He was very specific about the number. That was the number. I thought of saying to him, "You're telling me that, by the end of 2014, you need us to produce another 6,679 units?" But I sort of felt he wouldn't get it. Anyway, the point was that this was the most conservative estimate based on current orders and demand. Up to this point we had been self-financing, which was slow and difficult. "Maybe you need to raise capital," he said.

"Okay, maybe we will," I said.

"Or what?"

"Maybe we find a strategic partner."

I guess it was around this time that he started to drift. Maybe he was struggling with the stress. I just didn't know it until the Norway disaster. Milt just flat-out dropped the ball. He got the ratio of orange to blue doors all mixed up. It doesn't sound much but it threw out the numbers and put the preorder with the distributor at risk. They wanted out, and I had to eat massive humble pie and throw discounts around like they were confetti to get them back on board. It was one of the few times I really yelled at him. "Are you fucking deranged? How could you get it this wrong?"

I guess I should have known: he was looking for another job. He explained why. His Latvian wife was pushing him to earn more money. She didn't think I was paying him enough. Apparently she said, "When I met you, I thought, I've met my millionaire. So why aren't you, yet?" Harsh. It was bound to have an impact.

A valuable tip from the Professor (from his 13 Personal Habits that Have Helped Me Build Nine-Figure Businesses): "Make sure staff feel connected to their own development and their role in the overall goal and business." Milt was becoming disconnected. "How about this," I said. "If we sell to one of the big guys, I will pay you $400,000." That was enough of a connection, surely! "How does that sound?"

"Generous," he said. "But are you going to sell?"

"I don't know, but if you walk now you're liable to miss out on a big payday."

"Okay, let me think about it."

"I can offer you 2 percent of the equity."

"Two percent?"

"You'd be on what Alec Guinness was on for *Star Wars*. And that included merchandising. Everybody laughed then, but they're not laughing now."

The point is that a small percentage of a very large figure is still a very big paycheck. But even aside from that I honestly thought in my naive way that he would stay because we were like brothers. He was my amigo. He was my closest friend, as well as right-hand man. But he turned down the offer and left. He took up an offer from a bunch of guys on the West Coast and moved over there.

I was fairly broken up about it. All those years together, the games of table tennis, babysitting his kids while they went out to dinner: I couldn't believe Milt would do this to me. I would have taken a bullet for him, and he'd stabbed me in the back. In fact, I was going to leave Milt out of this story completely, just because the whole thing was too horrendous. But then again, since it happened, I thought I'd better put it in, painful or not. Minnesota Milt taught me the meaning of betrayal. I guess you're always learning.

When he left, it was like a great hairy iceberg just ripped a bloody great hole in the ship. But the miracle of it is that we didn't go down. If I may slightly misquote Spock, we fucked up and prospered.

Much later, Milt was sorry he'd done a runner. And his Latvian wife was furious.

41

THE GOD PARTICLE

A man's got to know his limitations

Right now subatomic particles are flying around a 16.8-mile circuit under Lake Geneva. At full speed, propelled by supercooled ultrapowerful magnets, traveling at 99.999 percent of the speed of light, they can do eleven thousand laps in a second. That's a marathon in one eleven-thousandth of a second. Our little ProDesk3D, though the fastest in its category, was not quite that fast.

All the time we were toiling away over a hot printer, the research scientists at the CERN Large Hadron Collider were intent on hunting down some new quantum phenomenon. It was not long since they had finally nailed the Higgs boson, otherwise known as "the God particle." In fact, now I come to think of it, botObjects was probably inspired by CERNian-style endeavor and especially the Higgs. I certainly was. The theory was that this one particle—or rather "field" as they say (so that the particle itself would be a "quantum excitation" of the field)—endowed all the other free-floating elementary particles with mass around the time of the Big Bang. Without the good old Higgs, we and the rest of the universe would be nothing other than a wannabe cloud of aging plasma. I suppose the upside would be that none of us would have a weight problem.

I had a notion of going over to CERN for a bit of a look-round, ultimately to inspect those elusive bosons and quarks at close quarters. I've always had a soft spot for cutting-edge pure research—I wasn't expecting any entrepreneurial opportunity; Higgs Inc, selling extra mass on the open market or extremely speedy particles in a jar. It's hard to compete with all that massive Euro lab tech and ridiculous expense account. But, unless I am totally deluding myself here, what we were doing at botObjects was not a million light-years away from the God particle. After all, were we not creating mass, making something out of nothing? Our printer was not just printing, it was giving birth to a brave new 3D world.

This was the fundamental excitement of owning a desktop 3D printer: you could play at being God. In the beginning, you created if not the heaven and the earth then at least a pair of shoes, a prosthetic limb, or an iPhone wallet. If we could sell enough of them and they became a mass phenomenon, then soon 3D objects would take over, and we would have a self-generating DIY realm, a parallel universe that could compete with the old one. Maybe, in the end, assuming unlimited progress, the 3D printer could come up with a new genesis, a better earth, more like heaven, improve on the original, and eradicate some of the flaws inherent in the first draft. Flip on the power button: let there be light, again!

It was a beguiling vision, and so far as I could make out there was only one problem. But it was a tough one, and I couldn't see a way around it. I found myself waking up—in those rare times when I managed to get some sleep—worrying about how to find a solution. So I took it to Tom. If anyone had the answer, he did. I found him in our basement lab: it wasn't CERN, but we definitely had our share of eureka moments and great breakthroughs down there. Tom was seated at a bench, bending over what looked like a heap of junk, but was almost certainly crucial bits of tech.

"I've been thinking about it ever since that day we printed out Cujo," I said.

"The little dog?" He looked up from his workbench and took off his glasses.

"See, that's the point. It's not a dog, it's only a model of a dog, a canine allusion. A canoid patch of color. Nothing like the real thing."

"I can do you a robot dog."

"Would it have the kind of legs that drop off?"

"So you want a living, breathing, barking dog?"

"I've probably got enough actual dogs, to be honest. And don't they say the dog population needs to be reined in anyway? But if you think about it, there's a fundamental problem of materials."

Tom nodded thoughtfully. "Yeah, you'd need a lot of hair, a nose, a tail, that sort of thing."

"Not to mention the soul of a new dog."

"I've got one of those somewhere," says he, looking around the lab.

I wouldn't put it past him to have a drawer with a label on it saying just that. He was a frustrated Dr. Frankenstein at heart. "But you see what I'm driving at?"

"Of course," he says. Pause. "But why don't you spell it out for me to be on the safe side?"

"What's our core raw material? Plastic. I know there's a variety of polymers we could be using. And it all makes sense because it's easy to shape. Even if it is a disaster for the planet. But I'm starting to feel that, in an ideal world, we wouldn't be limited to plastic."

"What did you have in mind?"

"Well, there's chocolate of course."

"Yes, like that printer that produces perfect brownies and M&M's. We could do that."

"What about rubber? We could do with a bit of flex."

"No problem."

"Metal?"

"Well, it's got to be soluble—that's going to require a high temperature but still, in principle . . ."

"What about wood?"

"Easy," says Tom. "If you get the right stuff."

"You know how our printer does all these different colors?"

"Full-color—our USP!"

"Well, could we do a printer that switches around from plastic to rubber to metal to wood and all that?"

"All in one machine?"

"All in one. Like the four elements—you know, earth, air, fire and water."

"Impossible," says he straight off the bat. "You're talking alchemy."

"I've been thinking—unless you can do that, you can't really make meaningful products, can you? You can't reproduce real stuff, because it's usually a mix of different materials, isn't it? Like a dog."

Tom reckoned he could design a printer that could use one or other of these different source materials but not one that did all of them simultaneously and could easily switch around. Consider a car, for example: Would you want an all-plastic car? An all-plastic ship or a plane? It would be like flying Spirit all the time. You'd need steel, maybe silver or gold.

"I can only think of two main obstacles," says Tom.

"Which are?" I was almost hopeful for a moment.

"Physics and chemistry."

I left him to get on with a more realistic and yet still quite epic undertaking—getting another 3D printer fully operational.

It was clear to me that, despite all our innovations, we needed another transcendent layer of innovation on top to stay ahead of the game. Fundamental truth: ultimately, everything always goes wrong. The ProDesk3D was a bit more precarious than that. It felt like being poised on a pinhead in a stiff wind with an earthquake going off. In order to get our printer working smoothly we had to achieve a level of molecular engineering we hadn't attempted before. It had to be absolutely perfect or it was a bust. Okay, we could live with that. We had been young enough and stupid enough to think we could do anything.

But now, if we wanted to go forward, we merely had to out-maneuver the boundaries of physics and chemistry, as Tom put it so neatly. We would require a nozzle the size of a Gatling gun. We had solved a thousand and one problems, and yet now we needed Newton, Einstein, Stephen Hawking, and Tom O'Brien to put their heads together to get us to the next level and build a genuine mass market. Of course it could be done, it would be done—in time. But we didn't have the resources of CERN. We were a classic hand-to-mouth, bootstrapping, fly-by-the-seat-of-your-pants, make-it-up-as-you-go-along, early-days startup. We were fueled more than anything by raging optimism. We had had the romance, but now we needed an injection of realism. We didn't know what we didn't know. We had run out of answers.

I am a geek at heart. I was fairly sure that all the other geeks out there shared my vision of a new installment of the Book of Genesis. That's what they were buying into. But what happened when they realized that there were limits? The God particle and my gut instinct were telling me that we were at peak hype, maximum fantasy—and the only way was down. Everything we had been doing so far had been floated upward by a soaring, manically enthused stock market, at least where 3D printer stocks were concerned. We had been flying. But what if, Icarus-like, we flew too close to the sun? We needed a rocket ship and all we had was feathers. The whole market was overdue, as they say, for "a correction"—in other words, a crash was imminent. There was a phrase of Clint Eastwood's, in *Dirty Harry*, that kept coming back to me. One of his ex-colleagues turned adversary has just been blown to smithereens by a car bomb: "A man's got to know his limitations."

One surprising thing I had discovered about the Higgs boson: the God particle doesn't last for very long. It emerges out of a high-speed collision and then decays and splits up after a fraction of a nanosecond. Well short of eternity. Our botObjects had had a lot longer existence than that, but perhaps we too were reaching the end of the road. When I looked at the tracks left by ephemeral particles in a bubble chamber, I was always reminded of one of those great Jackson Pollock paintings where he spread the canvas on his garage floor and emptied paint pots all over it. If you go to his place on Long Island you can still see a few drips and splashes, particles of paint on the garage floor. I also remember that Jackson Pollock finished his last great masterpiece, knocked back another drink, then hopped in his Oldsmobile, and sped off, zigzagging down the road. And he didn't make it to New York.

42

THE BEGINNING OF THE END

"You might be open to an early exit opportunity,"
says the Professor.

One simple fact you need to know that puts it all in context is this: in 2013 MakerBot was sold to Stratasys for $400 million. A tidy sum. To be honest, it probably planted a seed in my mind even in our very early stages.

Stratasys was the closest thing to Mimetics3D; MakerBot, run by Bre Pettis and based in Brooklyn, specialized in "desktop" printers. There are some obvious common denominators, but there was some big differences too. MakerBot had been around for several years. They had not just dreamed up an innovative product, but they had tried and tested and delivered. There was no talk of scams or hoaxes or crooks. They were bona fide, solid, reliable, with a proven track record. I imagine, if they had ever registered on the Trustpilot radar, they would have earned a stellar 4.8 or 4.9.

But you would have to say, all the same, that $400 million was a very decent price for a modest company. This was the golden age of acquisitions. A point that was not lost on Riley Griffin at Mimetics3D.

He was going around picking up companies the way a bee collects pollen.

Meanwhile, I was stressing out, as usual. We just couldn't produce our units fast enough. And the ones we did produce had a habit of going wrong. It must have been around this time that I took a call from one particularly irate distributor in Liverpool, England. "NONE OF THEM WORK!" he said, if you can use "said" for a guy who is speaking in capital letters. This could be one of those rare times where the verb "bellow" could apply.

I thought for probably the hundredth time, Jack should be taking this call. And in fact Jack had taken the call but he had then passed it on to me, as if it was all my responsibility. "You had better take this one," he said, a phrase that never failed to fill me with dread. We had sent this guy—let's call him Steve—a dozen printers. He was down for fifty, but we didn't have fifty, so I thought a few would keep him happy. And they might have satisfied him for a while, if not for the small problem that Bob was now drawing my attention to. "THEY'RE ALL BROKEN!" Capital letters and exclamation marks. Bellowed.

"That can't be quite right, surely," I responded. "It's not possible." I had sent out an entire battalion of troops and now Bob was telling me they had all been massacred. I couldn't believe it. There had to be a few survivors.

I asked for photos and further details. Two or three really were smashed. Clearly, our packaging still wasn't quite cutting the mustard. It didn't matter how many "FRAGILE" stickers you stuck on the box, it was still going to be used for throwing practice. And given that it was around the size of a small fridge, it presented an interesting challenge to the more adventurous of the baggage handlers—something like tossing the caber.

But the other failures were down to a simple technical issue. We had used the same power pack on the US machines as the ones we were sending to the UK. Big mistake. Nothing that works on one side of the Atlantic ever works on the other side. It took us about a week to source the right power packs and switch them over and get the other printers up and running. And thereby get Steve from Liverpool off my back. Another learning experience: don't trust the bright spark at the factory who tells you that power packs are universal.

I repeat what I've already said: Despite the capital letters and the exclamation marks, we never lost a single distributor (even if some were royally pissed off). Hiroshi went so far as to say, "This (the ProDesk3D) is the hope of Japan!" He was relying on it to save Japan from their economic woes, to print a renaissance in tech innovation. He truly believed. It remained true, however, that we had a failure rate of around 20–30 percent—way too high. We had produced a supersensitive 3D printer whose continued well-being hung by a thread. And I knew exactly what that felt like. I was still perplexed and weighed down by the big question, how could we scale up?

We could buy our way out of it—but the reality was that even if we unwrapped the entire $15.5 million rescue package, we were still looking at a three-year journey to get where we needed to go.

And then I got another call from Mimetics3D. In fact, three calls. I was in London when I picked up the messages. And I was more or less at my wits' end. So I called them back. This time it was the Strategic Development Department. I told them we could be interested in discussing a "partnership," but since it was the CEO of botObjects calling, perhaps it would be useful for me to talk directly with the CEO of Mimetics3D?

The next day I got a call from Riley Griffin. He wanted us to meet. "You're in New York, aren't you?" he said.

"Lafayette Street," I said.

"Cool, I'll come by your office."

This was the alternate solution, a potential Plan B. We had promised the world a brand-new 3D printer. Forty-something countries had already bought it. It could be as big as the PC. We had something that everybody was going to want. But maybe we could get someone else to deliver it for us? The ProDesk3D was our baby, and we desperately wanted it to succeed—but maybe adopted parents could do a better job?

I met Tom the next day in New York to talk it over. "Do you mean I wouldn't have to slog my guts out day and night any more, trying to keep the show on the road?" You could say he was reasonably enthusiastic about Plan B. Relief was probably his principal emotion. With a dash of joy. But the price had to be right. And we had to know that they were going to maximize and optimize our original vision—we weren't just going to take the money and run.

Tom was also concerned about giving away our secrets to a competitor. "How do we know they're not going to steal all our ideas?"

"It's like a striptease," I said. "You don't walk in there naked. Just give them a glimpse." Or, as the Professor puts it, *If the business model is so unique, supports excellent customer traction, and a key partner comes on, you might be open to an early exit opportunity should you consider it.*

43

CAN I TAKE HIM, OR CAN HE TAKE ME?

Are you feeling lucky, punk?

Riley Griffin was not a big man. Slightly sub–Tom Cruise, I would guess. With a short neck. But he was not short on chutzpah. He was not a young man, but he wore a leather bomber jacket and jeans, like the leader of the pack or, at a stretch, Marlon Brando in *The Wild One*. And he aggressively chewed gum. He was a little overweight, but he carried the extra pounds with the confidence that said yes, they really ought to be there, and they're all muscle. He didn't quite say that he was or ought to be ruler of the world, but he was probably thinking it.

He was wearing a pink 3D-printed watch that, alas, looked a little bit clunky, as if made by a brash kid in Queens rather than done with finesse by classy Swiss watchmakers. It reminded you, if anything, that 3D printers still had a way to go. Rolex wasn't panicking just yet.

I couldn't help thinking, looking at his pink watch, that none of us had got much beyond the pink whistle. I think it was the pink watch that was the tipping point for me: I felt like Muhammad Ali—"That all you got, Griffin?" In the back of my mind, the word "bubble" was starting to bubble up.

"This is the ProDesk3D," I said, proudly.

"I recognize it from Fox News," he said. "I wish I knew how you got all the publicity." He was the big kahuna, and we were the new kids on the block, but Riley was jealous of the attention we were getting.

"I wish I knew how you got the TED Talk." Subtext: When I saw Riley's TED Talk, I had two equal and opposite reactions: 1. He's saying what we think; 2. I don't really believe him because he's laying it on so thick—I mean, I was all in favor of "revolutionizing" manufacturing and bringing 3D to biotech and medical care and nutrition and education, and making your next pair of glasses or shoes whatever, but Riley's wild-eyed enthusiasm made me doubt what I originally thought. Would everyone "become an expert maker" as he maintained? Doubtful. He ended by saying, "I am a cobbler too" (like one of his ancient relatives); but his phrase called to mind an old British expression, "talking cobblers" (i.e., bullshit).

Tom had two printers going (yes, both barrels fully functional—I told you we had solved all the problems, didn't I?). They were churning out a string of tchotchkes, a teddy bear, a shoe, a vase, a rabbit's head, a skull, a miniature Taj Mahal, completely pointless items, but they were as colorful as a tub load of M&Ms. He was rubbing it in. We had color, and they didn't. They couldn't do what we could do.

"I like what I see, gentlemen," Riley said, stroking one of our printers. "I'd like to explore our options. I'm in town for a couple of days." He invited us to breakfast the following morning at the Plaza, where he was staying, on 5th Avenue across from Central Park.

I tried to work out what game Riley was playing. There was something about the way his eyes moved that made you feel you were being conned, even if you really weren't. He appeared completely transparent and, at the same time, I had a sneaking feeling he had something up his sleeve.

The fact was that he was going about with a big shopping bag and stuffing other companies into it like there was going to be a sudden shortage. He had, for example, acquired one company that printed chocolate. Maybe he would be printing croissants next or pancakes. Or burgers. None of it was impossible, none of it was ridiculous, but it wasn't clear that he had a plan beyond bulking up like some fanatical bodybuilder. He had certainly negotiated a lot of stock options along the way, and every acquisition pumped up the share price, so there was presumably a vested interest. But more than that, he had an almost imperialist, Napoleonic appetite for gobbling up territory that wasn't already his. He wanted to occupy the 3D space exclusively. And we were squarely in his sights. He had already made his mind up. He was like Wimpy in front of a pie.

Meeting Riley for the first time, I remembered something that Bertrand Russell once said. Somebody asked him what he first thought of on being introduced to another philosopher. His answer was: "Can I take him, or can he take me?"

44

BREAKFAST AT THE PLAZA

With all acquisitions, the entrepreneur's and the acquirer's major concerns will ultimately converge. The entrepreneur beyond seeking the highest price will want to minimize their exposure to any risks post-completion. The acquirer, on the other hand, will want to acquire what they want at the lowest possible price and will also seek to avoid any hidden risks and liabilities that the venture may be carrying. (The Professor)

"Do you have any 3D chocolate to put on my pancakes?" I thought I ought to ask, considering his acquisition history.

"We have chocolate sprinkles," said the waitress.

"Don't worry," says Riley, "all this will be 3D generated in the future, including the pancakes."

Even if it was cooked rather than printed, breakfast at the Plaza was everything breakfast at the Plaza ought to be. Tom and I agreed beforehand that we wouldn't stuff our faces so much we couldn't focus on the job at hand. There was so much on offer, it was a real cornucopia, but I tried to stick with the toast mainly. Riley was having eggs Benedict with extra bacon.

"Gentlemen," says Riley (I liked that—he always called us "gentlemen"), "we are building a vision. We are inventing the future right now, isn't that beautiful?"

"Beautiful," I agreed. Riley was like me, a visionary, just more gung-ho about it, maybe because he had only ever been in additive technology.

"So we can work together to make it happen? I can give you manufacturing, I can give you distribution, I can give you customers, I can give you financing."

There was a lot of "giving," which sounds all right, but the subtext was that he wanted something for nothing. I didn't want to give away everything we had worked on in exchange for breakfast at the Plaza. "Tom and I," I said carefully, "have discussed the options and we think it would be better to think in terms of a merger."

Riley put his cup of coffee down. "What is your ideal outcome?" Now we were getting down to it.

"One hundred and fifty million," I said. Keep it plain. Don't hedge it around with "I think" or "we estimate" and all that. Obviously we had done our sums (what the Prof calls "determination of assets of value"). And it was a fraction of the MakerBot price. He didn't need to see the workings too.

"No one is going to pay that kind of money," he said, with something like a "ha!" or an ironic laugh. "Not too many CEOs will come and meet you for breakfast."

When he said that it made me wonder: Did he know I had called Stratasys? After speaking to Riley that first time I had put a call through to his opposite number at Stratasys. Turned out the CEO was on holiday for a couple of weeks and had given strict orders not to be contacted. My visions of a mass Dutch auction went out the window and ended up on a beach in Tahiti or somewhere. We had no one else out there to support the price. It was breakfast at the Plaza or nothing.

It's important not to sound too grateful. I said, "You're not going to meet too many CEOs for breakfast with a world-leading product on the table."

"I think the Plaza pancakes are good too, but I'm not paying 150 million."

"What sort of price did you have in mind?"

"I was thinking more like 25 million. That would be a fair price."

"Tom and I agreed we would consider 100."

At this point Mrs. Griffin made an entrance. Riley hopped up to greet her and did the intros. She looked at us shrewdly and said, "I can see you're busy—I'm going to investigate the buffet."

"What would I do without her?" Riley said.

"It's all about the teamwork," I said.

"I think we're going to converge on fifty."

I looked at Tom. He looked back at me. "I don't know. We're going to have to talk it over."

45

MAKE YOUR MIND UP

Tom says, "Take the money and run."

I'm a binary sort of guy. And it was a simple binary choice in the end: build or sell. This would be a much longer book, and in fact would not even have an ending if we had gone for growth. Tom and I trooped back to Lafayette Street.

"We have prior art," I said. "We have the patents. He has to use them or destroy them. He can't work around them."

"We've been going at this for only a year or so," says Tom. "Fifty million seems like a decent return."

"And don't forget his printers are the size of sofas. Huge sofas. They're industrial, not consumer. Maybe we should wait for Stratasys."

"Let's take the money and run."

"We're worth more. Are they going to look after our baby? Are they good custodians?"

"It's still a great deal. Make your mind up."

Tom had a point. Seventy percent of startups fail within five years; after ten years it's more like 90 percent. Only around 1 percent manage to sell. Whatever happened, we were sitting pretty. We didn't need to drag it out.

So we slept on it and then went for breakfast at the Plaza for the second day in a row. But it felt more like *High Noon*. The final showdown.

"Tom and I agree that $50 million is an acceptable price."

Riley held out his hand and I took it. "Shall we do half liquid and half in stock options?"

I had a notion he was going to say that. Stock options are great if the price is still going up. And the Mimetics3D price would go up immediately after this acquisition, no doubt about that. But what was the longer-term picture? Riley's pink watch suggested I should be cautious. Maybe not everybody wanted a pink watch—or a pink whistle. "We would rather keep it simple," I said. "Fifty million is 50 million."

Riley gritted his teeth. It was almost a snarl. "Then it's a deal."

I inwardly breathed a deep sigh of relief.

"Always providing," he said, adding a rider that filled me with anxiety all over again, "you can come down to Fort Mill—"

"No problem," I said.

"—and let the team get to grips with your printer."

Nothing was agreed until everything was agreed. We had had breakfast, but no cigar.

46

DELIVERANCE

The little problem at Dunkin' Donuts in North Carolina

I don't know if you've seen *Deliverance*—the seventies classic in which a bunch of city boys (including Jon Voight, Burt Reynolds, and Ned Beatty) head off into the country for an adventure and end up being chased, raped, or murdered by a gang (or family?) of mad hillbillies, somewhere in the South. Well, this was like the sequel. The guy had a mullet cut, a big bushy beard, and tattoos everywhere. And a bunch of broken, missing, or brown teeth. I could see them quite well because he was standing right in front of me when he said, "I'm going to get you." Which was unsettling to say the least. Particularly when I had seen *Deliverance* about three times and every frame of it was etched into my memory. Especially the nonconsensual parts.

I had already started to think this road trip was a big fat mistake several hours previously. This just about settled it: we should have taken the plane after all. The problem was that the turbulence was looking bad. As you know, it's not that I'm afraid of getting on a plane. Not at all. I love the flying machine and even now am developing an all-electric vertical-takeoff vehicle. But I do hate turbulence. I just don't fancy being shaken up and down like a martini.

Tom and I had agreed to meet Riley down in Fort Mill in a couple of days. He flew back there. "Let's get the flights booked," says Tom. But when I looked at the charts I could see nothing but trouble brewing. It was like tapping the barometer and the needle swings round to "STORMY WEATHER."

"Could you fancy a road trip?"

"M, it must be a thousand miles!"

"A mere 652."

"That's about twelve hours' driving. And back again."

"We can drive through the night," I said. "It'll be fun!"

"You're mad."

"Think about the printers then. We have to take two. What are the chances of them being broken before we arrive?"

"We put VERY FRAGILE stickers on—they'll be fine."

"You know how well that works. Remember Tokyo?"

"Add extra Styrofoam."

"Tom, we can't take the chance—if we hit turbulence we're sunk."

"It's on you if we get hijacked or crash."

"I'll do most of the driving, okay?"

One way or another, we had to go. We still didn't have the "LOI," the Letter of Intent. All we had was a handshake. We had been reasonably relaxed and fatalistic about a deal before. But now there was $50 million on the table. We weren't quite so relaxed any more. Even the LOI was only illustrative, it wasn't binding, but it would be enough to get the lawyers working on the deal. We had to get the LOI—and for that we needed the ProDesk3D to be on top form. It had to be infallible, like the Pope. But, as usual, it wasn't.

We packed the two printers down tight in the back of the Range Rover, like we were tucking in two of our babies for the night. The road trip started out well enough, even though it was one of those early starts, around 4 a.m. We talked strategy and we also talked about what we were going to do with $50 million. We agreed that $50 million was a decent return on just over a year's work. I was the majority shareholder, but Tom had enough that we weren't going to fall out over a few million. "I can't believe we're really doing it," says Tom.

"It's the right thing to do," I said, "if we want to take the risk out. Mimetics3D are the world leaders. They're a ten-billion-dollar company. They have way more capital than we do. They have manufacturing and retail outlets all sewn up. They'll do a good job."

We kept on rolling for as long as possible, but we had to stop and refuel and get out and stretch our legs somewhere in North Carolina. On a deserted stretch of road between Durham and Greensboro. There was some kind of issue on the main road and a diversion took us way off, deep into the country. It was a little place with no name and only a gas station and a Dunkin'. We were going to stop at the gas station, and we actually pulled in, but it was so dark and deserted and scary-looking, like something out of a Jeffrey Dahmer documentary, we went: Fuck no! Drive on! No point in taking stupid chances. "If we get out, we won't get back in," said Tom, memorably. And so we came to the Dunkin' Donuts (as it was then, now just Dunkin'). How could that go wrong? It's a Dunkin' Donuts, ffs!

"Come on," says Tom, "let's get you a coffee or you'll be nodding off at the wheel."

Which is when we bumped into the hillbilly. Or several hillbillies, as a matter of fact. It was just the one bearded dude, hair shaven at the sides, receding on top and way too long at the back, who stepped across me and said he was going to "get" me. Only me, mark you, not Tom. He had a ton of tattoos all over his arms and on his neck all the way up his ears. I may have forgotten to look at them all that closely but I imagine they included skulls, a scaffold, and assorted poetic statements such as F.U.C.K. and H.A.T.E. (and possibly K.I.L.L. for all I know). A lot of tattoos, not so many teeth. My first impression was that he was a meth addict. That didn't change too much in the course of our relationship. Maybe he cooked crystal meth for a living.

"Why would you want to do that?" I asked, genuinely mystified.

"I don't like the way you're looking at me," says tattooed dude.

I thought of explaining to him that the only reason I was looking at him was that he had got in my way and told me he was going to get me. But I thought better of it. For one thing, he might not like the smart-ass answering-back routine. For another, his numerous friends who had all swiveled around to register my existence might not like it either. They looked the kind of guys who owned shotguns and were dead set on asserting their Second Amendment rights to use them. I would estimate there were eight or nine of them. Fellow meth-cookers.

"Your coffee," says the Dunkin' guy.

"Excuse me," said I, pointing at the coffee, and edging around the obstacle. "Getting coffee." It was the best I could come up with at the time.

Tom and I sat down at a table. But Beardy and his hillbilly crew were still giving us the eye. There was something about being under surveillance by the country boys that quelled all our merry talk of how we were going to spend 50 million. Not only had they sucked all the excitement out of us—at this point I wasn't too sure we were going to get out of North Carolina alive. "I'm going to the bathroom," I said. Then, under my breath, "Tom, follow me in a minute, okay?"

He nodded mutely.

"We've got to get out of here."

As I had hoped, the restroom was at the back of the restaurant. Also as I hoped, there was a window. And, yes, it was just about big enough for Tom and me to scramble through and run back to the car. We got in, and I fumbled nervously with the ignition.

The boys must have been missing us, because six of them came running out after us. I jammed my foot down and took off. Looking into my rearview mirror, I could see them jump into two pickups and come storming after us. Armed to the teeth, probably. I thought I could hear the dread sound of massed pump-action shotguns being loaded. Fortunately this was not *Duel*. My Range Rover was recently serviced and now fully fueled. It was more than a match for a couple of ancient Chevies. It wasn't until I had put miles and miles between us and got back on the main road to Charlotte that I finally breathed a sigh of relief.

"What is it about you that winds people up?" says Tom after a while. Like it was my fault or something.

"I guess they're just jealous," I said.

"Maybe they don't like your glasses."

"I always thought they make me look like Buddy Holly."

"I told you we should fly," he said.

Really, there is no end to the potential for turbulence.

47

THE DOLL'S HOUSE

Small is beautiful?

Coming within an ace of getting murdered and perhaps worse may explain why it was we took a taxi the next morning. Plus I didn't want to have to find the place and I just didn't fancy driving any more. We had the two printers on our laps, Tom in the back and me in the front.

You could say the woman driver was laid back. She had the seat folded so far down that she could hardly see over the dashboard. More of her was in the back of the car than in the front. And she had the grindingly slow southern drawl.

"Tom," I said when we got out at Mimetics3D, "we're going to have to adjust. It's a different culture. This is like a whole new world down here. We need to talk slow."

We had planned it all out in the cigar room at the hotel the night before, like a couple of generals in front of maps the night before battle. Victory was inevitable, we thought. But this was before a shot had been fired. The reality was we had no idea what we were walking into.

Riley met us and took us into a conference room and made the intros. There must have been around fifteen of them. We were outnumbered. I don't know if it was the effect of the hillbillies or the laid-back lady taxi driver, but I had this weird feeling that they were all aliens, as per *Men in Black*, just masquerading as CTOs and lawyers and marketing and PR people. It seemed like we had driven out of New York and landed on another planet. Fortunately there was one guy there who didn't seem like a member of the alien inquisition. Rick Bull was not only a legend of 3D printing, but a friendly, decent guy in his early seventies with white hair, a broad smile, and a firm handshake. He gave me renewed confidence that we would be okay. "I want to give you only one small thing to print out," says Rick. No problem! I say to myself. Yes, we can! "A miniature doll's house."

Wtf? I nearly spat out my coffee when I looked at the STL file (which shows the printer exactly what to print across all three dimensions and chops it all up into neat bite-sized slices). He wasn't kidding about the "miniature"—it was about 3 by 2 inches. And everything in the doll's house was minute: minute figures, minute chairs, and minute tables. And even minuter teapot and cups. This was like nano-printing. All our efforts, and it had all come down to this mission fucking impossible.

"Can you do that okay?"

"Sure," said Tom. "It might take a little while." He was great at not showing emotion and he could spin a positive story without actually lying. (Funnily enough I asked him about it later: one word he used stuck in my mind—"dread." He thought it was going to be "really really tough" but he could "have a shot at it.")

I put a brave face on it. "I can answer any questions you have," I said, "while the printer is printing."

I had no idea if our little printer was up to it. I had a sudden vision of $50 million walking out of the door and vanishing into the South Carolina wilderness. I tried my best to bottle that thought up as I fielded the questions.

"What are your printer's weaknesses?"

"Can you achieve the full rainbow?"

"Are you the fastest?"

"Can you really do twenty-five microns?"

"There's no way you can print at that speed and get the object cool enough."

They were coming thick and fast. I felt hot in my blazer even though the air-conditioning was throbbing. There was even a question about the tri-fan architecture. "We don't have a patent on that," I conceded. "But it's an innovation we need in order to cool the nozzle, and under it and behind it, given that it's going so fast and sequencing all the colors. And don't forget we have twelve motors, six for the cartridges, three for the nozzle, one to get it up and down, and another two for the fans: it's on a different level." We had all the answers. I told them emphatically we could print any object at any temperature with any colors.

Meanwhile I could hear the printer chugging away behind me. All twelve motors firing. So far so good. It was working. And we were withstanding the bombardment. Riley broke up the meeting for coffee, and he and his crew went out of the room to consult. Which is when Tom tapped me on the shoulder.

"I think you should have a look at this," he said. There was something in the way he said it that froze my blood.

"Looks good to me," I said, surveying the front of the doll's house.

"Now look at the back," he says.

I walked around the printer and inspected the doll's house from the rear. Sure enough there it was: the walls were peeling. The doll's house was starting to melt like an ice cream in the sun. We were stuffed. All our work had been for nothing, all because of a shitty little miniature doll's house. The whole journey, from the pink whistle all the way to Fort Mill, flashed before my eyes. And it was all in vain. No doll's house, no 50 million, no nothing. The deal was dead.

Riley and his crew trooped back in. "How's it going, Martin?" says he, brightly.

I didn't know if he had seen what we had seen or not. "Looks like we've run into a small problem," I admitted.

Rick Bull came over and inspected. He folded his arms and nodded. "You know, none of our printers can print that either."

"You haven't?"

"It's basically impossible. Maybe with an industrial printer, if you go down to ten microns. Not with twenty-five."

So he had set us up to fail. He expected us to fail. But, perhaps, as Samuel Beckett would say, we had "failed better." Maybe they were just letting us sweat, to see how we would cope under pressure. We were still standing.

"So do you think you still want our printer?"

"I think we do," he said.

Two days of hard negotiating and one celebratory dinner later, we drove away with the LOI in our hands.

This is helpful from the Professor: "Quick definition: A letter of intent (LOI) outlines the terms of a deal. It serves as an 'agreement to agree' between two parties. An LOI is used in most acquisition transactions of any material value."

That's okay, then isn't it?

"Secondly, another goal is to identify any potential risks, downsides, or problems that can be factored into the final buy-sell agreement, or enable each party to walk away."

Fuck!

48

SIXTY DAYS

Do you remember what we did with the receipts?

"You look like you've seen a ghost." So said Norman in the armchair next to me. When we got back to New York, I rushed off to my cigar club and took one out of the humidor. I needed to recover.

"I've just driven over 1,200 miles," I said, lighting up. "Over twenty-four hours at the wheel."

"Oh yeah, how did it go down south?" he said. I had happened to tell Norman all about Fort Mill before setting off. "I thought you'd be coming back with a nice tan."

I inhaled deeply and breathed out a careworn cloud of smoke. "I think we just got beaten up."

And I wasn't talking about any hillbillies either.

I know, I know: we had the LOI. Mission accomplished, you could say. Hadn't everything gone according to plan? Yes, but the drive back north rapidly turned into a nightmare. It started well and then spiraled into a deep pit of anxiety and foreboding. Driving 1,200 or 1,300 miles can do that to you. I resolved to take the plane next time, turbulence or no. But it wasn't that. It was more the worrying about the next sixty days. We had agreed, John Thompson—their chief legal officer—and I, that sixty days would be the deadline to close the deal. Or not. But either way, no more than sixty. For starters, you can end up paying a fortune in legal fees if you're not careful; but more than that, you have to keep up the momentum—if you let too much time go by you're likely to get left high and dry and meanwhile you've been massively distracted from the job of steering the company. But even so, a lot can go wrong in sixty days. And there was a lot to go wrong, we increasingly realized.

As you can imagine, Tom and I set out from Fort Mill on a glorious sunny day with coffees in our hands and broad smiles on our faces, elated and congratulating ourselves on a deal well done. "Smart work, partner!" "Couldn't have done it without you, man!" "Teamwork makes the dream work!" All that sort of thing. Like a couple of surfers who have just surfed the wave of their lives. We were full of ourselves, making phone calls to our wives boasting about what great negotiators we were. Patting ourselves on the back. Like it was already a done deal.

Then, slowly but surely, a sense of reality started creeping back in as we found ourselves reliving all the highs and lows—but especially the lows—of the last fifteen months. Because it was the lows that Mimetics3D would be looking at—a long trail of them, like Neanderthal footprints locked visibly into some ancient track. From here on in, we were under scrutiny. It was like being audited by the Spanish Inquisition. Otherwise known as "due diligence." The deal was anything but done.

Something I always tell my entrepreneurship students: don't cut corners! Get yourselves a proper accountant! One of these days I need to start listening to my own advice. We did nothing but cut corners. "Do you remember what we did with the receipts?" I said, after a hundred miles or so.

"Do you?" says Tom, with the emphasis on *you*, which is to say, *me*.

It was my problem. I was supposed to be the one trained in accountancy. Lesson 1: Keep the receipts. Not everything, it would be fair to say, had been properly recorded. We tended to rely on petty cash for most transactions. The fact is we had been working at lightning speed and record-keeping tended to get, shall we say, de-prioritized. Buried would be another word. Neglected and postponed. Binned. We don't have time for that right now, was the attitude. Later! Now all our sins of omission were going to come back to haunt us. A major part of the deal was that Mimetics3D could now come and inspect our books to make sure they were all square. The reality was that the books were not square, they only had aspirations toward some kind of geometry, when they weren't blank.

What would the Professor say? *In one of my seminars, I talk about building the exit from the start, and what I mean is putting in the foundation for due diligence, starting with an accounting system.*

"They're going to peer into every crevice," I said to Tom. "They're going to give us the sharp intake of breath. And they're going to bring the price down or back out."

"Let me know what I can do," said Tom.

That felt like the longest road trip ever. Responsibility for the M&A had fallen on my shoulders. I really needed that cigar by the end of it.

I should have listened to the Professor, he knew what he was talking about: *Get ready for due diligence. Part of the exit checklist is the very important item of being prepared for due diligence.*

The War Room became the electronic data room in which they could access all our secrets. Which felt a little bit like being strip-searched. And there were about ten of them, snooping into our archives, excavating all our failures and limitations. Naturally, we wanted to draw attention to everything on our side that looked good; they were focusing on everything that looked bad. Every now and then our lawyer, Patrick, would drop by and look over their shoulders. "It's not looking good," he said ominously. "You've got so many holes. They're never going to agree to it. In fact, they could sue you." He didn't quite say, "I told you so," but it was close.

I thought the deal was dead.

We will go back to this later in the seminar series, but part of planning for the exit is to have your functional information well mapped out, organized and easily accessible. Tips to Avoid Pitfalls . . . That was the sound of the Professor kicking me in the butt. Often entrepreneurs will be moving so fast, that sometimes the internal processes get left behind, and then providing important documents at the due diligence stage becomes a problem. You can say that again, o wise one!

In principle, the idea is not to show any chinks in the armor. The weird thing is that we solved our financial documentation problem by being honest about it. Honesty saved us. There was no point to trying to cover up all our mistakes. When you know you're in the wrong, the important thing is to say it with confidence. I do it with my wife all the time. "Look," I said, "we can go back and trace all those missing receipts." In the end they weren't too bothered about a few holes. They still wanted the printer, warts and all. "It's not the end of the world," they said. "You were moving fast."

Same thing with the inventory. No responsible paperwork. We were fumbling in the darkness. Take it from me, this kind of being-too-smart-for-your-own-good will come back to bite you. It was like we were going for the world's land speed record and now the vehicle had just hit a bump in the road and gone into a spin. How many had we actually sold? What about all the distributor deals? Were any of them likely to evaporate? The Mimetics3D guys were going to call each of them up. To be honest, I was concerned about what some of them might say. "We're still waiting for those fucking printers!" "We want our money back!" That sort of thing. What happened was that Mimetics3D blew off all the distributors, gave them their money back, and worked with their own distribution system. So in the end it was no big deal. We had dodged another bullet.

The breakages issue? That was disposed of under the heading of "breakages." "Hey, everyone has breakages."

And our cybersecurity? "It's usually the Russians. Either that or bored teenage hackers in Cleveland."

But it was still sixty days of nerve-shredding hell. I was pacing and panicking: my Fitbit told me that I had walked fifteen thousand steps in one day. I must have worn out a few carpets. I knew that when you're a small company, one puff of wind in the wrong direction can blow you right out of the water.

In the midst of everything, John Thompson came over and took a look at all our patents. We had 106 of them. He spends hours poring over them then turns around and says to us, "I'm not sure they're all that valuable."

Fortunately I had the wisdom of the Professor to guide me here: *When assessing the competitors, it will be important to validate your USP's (unique selling points) against what your competitors are doing, so that you can isolate what you have to offer a potential acquirer and to be able to clearly articulate and substantiate this value.*

"Well," I said, "without them you don't have a viable full-color consumer printer. So it's up to you." The key thing is not to be too fazed by this kind of thing. It's normal. If they're buying you they want to beat you down. It's like selling a house or a car. The buyer will always try to find fault. It needs a new roof! Or the camshaft is shot! You just have to stand firm. Don't fall for the bullshit. If they want what you have, they are going to have to put up with a few scratches.

We gave them the usual warranties, indemnities, and guarantees (or WIGs for short). Considering we didn't have the data, we had to. (Professor: Some quick definitions: *Warranty: A warranty is a written guarantee, issued to the purchaser of the shares or assets. Indemnity: An indemnity is security against or exemption from legal liability for one's actions. Guarantee: A guarantee is written assurance from the entrepreneur that certain conditions will be fulfilled.*)

The deal was closed after sixty days, just as we had agreed. It felt like I'd done a PhD in a couple of months. I was probably as close to cracking up during that time as I've ever been. At one point I thought I was dying. I was in London reading over the hundreds of pages of the agreement (that they had drafted). I called up Tom: "Tom, I'm dying!" I said. In fact I think I died. But I recovered.

Could Gary have done it better? Yes.

Could Tom have done it better? Yes.

Could I have done it better? Absolutely. I promise to do better next time.

But in the end we signed on the dotted line. Mimetics3D and bot-Objects were now as one. Cue corks popping, hats flying. We had got the deal over the line. It was the biggest thing in our relatively young lives. It was official: We had just earned $50 million. And I had lost a lot of weight in the process.

BDD, Business Due Diligence, all done and dusted. But, looking back, maybe we should have been more concerned with CDD: contractual due diligence. Because right under our noses Riley was quietly stitching us up. He sold us a total work of fiction. Jordan Belfort (a.k.a. the Wolf of Wall Street) says, "it was the nature of twentieth-century capitalism that everyone should scam everyone." I don't think that's right, not about business in the twenty-first century either. We didn't scam anyone; we were scammed.

49

THE LAST CIGAR

Against company policy

"Get out here, we need to plan!"

We took the plane this time. Come on, it's Riley calling! It felt like emerging from a cave into the light. (I'm giving you a little flashback to the middle of our sixty-day waiting period.)

The thing about having dinner with Riley is that you're still negotiating all the way from the appetizer through to dessert and coffee. The haggling never stopped the whole time I knew him. It made the actual printing part of the whole thing seem relatively straightforward. Across the table I could see Tom still fielding questions from some of the managers. But I was sitting right next to Riley, and he had perfected the art of cutting, slicing, and dicing a deal even while chewing. He could eat dinner and talk percentages simultaneously. It was a perfectly decent restaurant in Fort Mill, but I had a feeling I was selling my soul to the devil. It was enough to give anyone indigestion.

The crux of it was: What would happen after the merger? Some of our staff were going to be squeezed out, that was certain. They would all get a parachute payment. But what about Tom and me in particular? They still needed us. The big idea was that we would become vice presidents of a dedicated botObjects division. The theory was that if we could sell enough of our machines, then we would be paid more than $50 million. So when you added it all up the grand total came to more like our original valuation of the company. That was the way the "share purchase agreement" was stacked up—so much on signature but then part payment in commission. But of course that depended on there being a lot of printers available to sell. But were there? And did they even have a sales plan? Riley had said they could produce fifty a day, but in reality it was more like fifteen, or five.

Yes, we had a whole division. Yes, we had job titles. And yes, we had made millions. But our baby had been adopted and we were, effectively, homeless. I had a bad feeling about it the time I lit a cigar in the old office on Lafayette. I had nearly given up. In fact I had given up after the cancer scare. It was like, okay, one last cigar. Purely symbolic. You have to understand, now I didn't own anything. I didn't own the TV on the wall. I didn't own the desk, I didn't own the chair I was sitting on, I didn't own the computer. I especially didn't own any printers. The only thing I was fairly sure I owned was my humidor. So I took out a classic Cuban cigar and lit up. It felt good. It tasted of jungle and samba. I started to think maybe a second life under the umbrella of Mimetics3D wouldn't be so bad after all.

"You're not allowed to smoke in this building." It was some guy from marketing.

"But I've always smoked in this building," I replied, genuinely mystified.

"It's against company policy."

"Well," I was about to object, "it sure as hell isn't my company policy."

But then it wasn't my company any more, was it?—it was Riley's company. We belonged to Mimetics3D now. That was the nature of the deal. I went out to smoke my cigar. The whole mad journey started with a cigar and it ended with one. I think it was then I realized I could be out any time.

But it didn't really hit home until the consumer electronics show at the convention center in Las Vegas. And I went up the steps of the Hawker 800.

50

THE HANGOVER

Are we being shafted?

We were excited, because we had done the deal and we had just joined forces with the Big Kahuna. "Controversial" little botObjects had finally been validated by the numero uno of 3D printing.

Riley told us what to expect—TV interviews, press, podcasts, the whole shebang. We were front-page news, he said. "It's gonna be massive!" We were starring at CES, and he had deliberately saved up the announcement to maximize the impact. It was our Big Bang moment. Of course, it wouldn't be botObjects without the usual last-minute crises. We sent four gleaming, immaculate, infallibly packed printers via San Francisco. None of them arrived. Tom went into panic mode and called up Dylan at 2 a.m.

"I need you to get on a plane."

"When?"

"Now!"

"From where?"

"An airport!"

"Yeah, but . . ."

Dylan had to pick up a couple more printers from Gary and get his ass over to Vegas in a hurry. But it was barely after Christmas and Dylan had only just gotten to bed, and he had been out drinking. He couldn't drive, physically or legally. After delivering a certain amount of justifiable abuse, Tom had to fork out $850 for a taxi to take Dylan to the airport via Gary in New Jersey before flying on to Las Vegas. In the end our original printers turned up in San Francisco, having detoured via Sydney, so we had a grand total of six printers all clacking away in Vegas.

The usual cock-ups and emergencies aside, we decided this was our moment of triumph, our day in the sun. Perhaps it was only a Warhol-style fifteen minutes of fame but we were going to milk it for all it was worth. We had to stage an entrance in style, as if we were Hollywood stars. We deserved a little of the red carpet treatment, didn't we? I would finally get to live out my Tom Cruise/Brad Pitt/George Clooney/Clint Eastwood fantasy. The check had landed after all. So naturally we took a private jet. Not something I do all the time. But surely allowable once in a blue moon. We flew in from London, via New York, so it wasn't cheap. And that was part of the point, after all. If you want to know, it would have set us back around $75k, plus extras. Madness, you will say, but we only did it once. And it all blew up in our faces.

I love Las Vegas. Even though I don't gamble, there's always something going on. And to be fair to Mimetics3D, we not only had will.i.am in full flow, we even had David Copperfield making some of our printers vanish. Which was very cool. Tom was staying at the Venetian, and I had the presidential suite at the Four Seasons Mandalay with my wife and daughter—billed, of course, to Riley Griffin. It was full-on five-star. I had even booked a separate suite at the Sands for all the press interviews and the film crews. Well, we wanted to look good on-screen, didn't we?

And, most importantly, the ProDesk3D—ProDesk3D plural!—had a prime spot at the Mimetics3D booth at the expo. Almost miraculously, they all worked (thank you, Tom). The only thing was it had been rebadged. Tom had had to rush around and get a new logo printed and stuck on the machine. Now and henceforth the artist formerly known as the ProDesk3D would be the CubePro Full-Color 3D Printer. Our printer, with the name up in lights, even if it wasn't exactly our name any more. Specifically for the show we had printed the most beautiful clocks, a spectacular sunburst yellow-orange one and a blue one, that were some of the best things we had done. And— get this—an eagle: I mean, a show-stealing eagle-sized eagle, with feathers. It could virtually fly. We even printed a couple of feathery iPhone cases to go with.

Which was all well and good. But the cold harsh fact was: I had absolutely nothing to do. Or say. I still had a job, I had the motivation, but I had been severely sidelined and silenced. I was just twiddling my thumbs at the show. Where were the press interviews, where was the spotlight? Nada. Our dedicated interview suite remained stubbornly unoccupied. We had been lured in with the offer of the part of Hamlet and here we were playing Rosencrantz and Guildenstern. Or a couple of lowly set painters. It was like we had been airbrushed out of the picture. We—the superstars of 3D printing—were benched. The guy who was recruited to talk up the CubePro knew as much about it as my granny. It was almost like they wanted to sink it. They didn't want us to say anything to anybody. They didn't trust us. David Copperfield and will.i.am had suddenly appeared and then vanished again, like short-lived, flaming meteors. The Vegas show was, in short, a sham, a fucking insult. Tom was laid back about it, as per usual: I was fuming. We had been marched up to the top of the hill then marched back down again.

"Enjoy your time in Las Vegas!" said Riley, when I asked him what the hell we were supposed to be doing. But I didn't really want a holiday in Vegas, blowing money on the tables and going to shows. All I wanted to do was let the world know how cool our printer was. But I was never given the chance. I couldn't get going soon enough. Maybe we had celebrated too soon.

Riley insisted on us taking one of the Mimetics3D jets. "Please," says he, "it's the least we can do."

"We already have a jet," says I, grandly.

"No problem. Fly with us and you can get credit on yours. I won't hear of you paying for it." Obviously, was the subtext, you're only hiring the jet, we actually own the jet.

"Deal." It would have been rude to reject the offer. We packed up and were driven to the airport.

Now, I have to say one thing. I am a lucky bastard even having access to a private plane, nicely paid for by Mimetics3D. It's for sure better than getting elbowed and hassled in the queue for a commercial flight and then squeezing into a seat. And, to reiterate, I wasn't even paying for the return journey. And, of course, we were $50 million richer. But still I have to register something that seemed to me significant at the time. It's subtle, but it rankled.

Tom stayed behind, saying he wanted to try out his "system" on the roulette table. He wasn't even too put out by the treatment in Las Vegas. "How do you feel about it?" I asked him. "Are we being shafted?" "You know what, I don't care anymore," says he. I guess I still cared. So it was me, my wife, and my daughter. We were driven right into a hangar where a beautiful, gleaming Gulfstream 650 in all its glory was parked. If you don't know, it's the Rolls-Royce, the crème de la crème, of business jets. It's a Kim Kardashian among planes. Room for seventeen to nineteen passengers. Full kitchen and bar and massive cinema screen. Not even Tom Cruise could ask for more. I breathed a sigh of relief that we were at least going to get a comfortable ride back to New Jersey. Maybe life at Mimetics3D wouldn't be so bad after all.

But what happened was this: the limo drove past slowly, not stopping, then kept on driving until we hit another hangar containing not a Gulfstream but a Hawker 800. An ancient Hawker 800, at least fifteen years old, cramped and miserable, a quarter the size of a Gulfstream. It was basically a rattling rust bucket—a joke. I had five hours of non-stop turbulence to look forward to on the flight back to Morristown. And it was embarrassing. My wife, who can put up with a lot, said, "Is that it?" She gave me a look as if to say, Wow! But not in a good way.

Then we saw the Gulfstream 650 taxi right past us, grandly, gloriously, with majestic indifference, as if to remind us of what we were missing.

Yes, it was better than driving the whole way, via hillbilly-land. But not by much. To me, it was a symbolic slap in the face. It was like being asked to use the tradesman's entrance. I was on my way out. The romance was over. As we flew back, I felt heartbroken. I couldn't even get the pulldown table to pull down, not while I was actually sitting there. This was supposed to be our lap of honor, our crowning moment—like standing on the podium at the end of *Star Wars* and getting a medal pinned to our chests, having done our duty by the Force. Instead of that it felt more like we were on the deck of the *Titanic* as it went under.

But, setting aside all the subtle symbolism of cigars and Gulfstreams, here is the fundamental fact: Riley misrepresented his company to *us*. We were worrying about being transparent and honest with him about botObjects. We didn't want to misrepresent anything. And all along he was conning us every which way about Mimetics3D. I've got to give Riley this—he was good at the spiel. Maybe too good.

They were supposed to be expanding production. In fact, they were shutting us down.

51

BUT THE UPSIDE WAS . . .

Not a hoax after all

Enough quibbling. It was a great deal.

Everything was signed and sealed on December 16. It felt like Christmas had come early that year. But we agreed not to make any public announcements until the trade show in January 2015.

Riley said how "thrilled" Mimetics3D were to acquire botObjects and "excited" to team up with Martin Warner and Tom O'Brien in order to "democratize" 3D printing. I said I was "joining a winning team" and I was looking forward to getting our "revolutionary" technology out there faster. The immediate explosion in the trade press was gratifying. It was all, "You were right and I was wrong." "I said it would never work. But what do I know?" "They must have had something we couldn't see." It was the heartwarming sound of humble pie being eaten across the nation.

Here's how one gobsmacked pundit, "The Voice of 3D Printing" (in 3Dprint.com, January 5, 2015), summed up our short history: "botObjects is a company that has provided a lot of hope within the consumer level 3D printing space. While this hope remained in the hearts of some, over the course of the past year to year and a half, that hope had begun to fade as many people who had preordered the company's printers began claiming that the botObjects was a scam." Well, considering we were only seventeen months old at the time of the merger, it seems on the face of it implausible that hope could have been fading for a year and a half. And the only people who said it was a scam turned out to be the biggest scammers of them all and were being paid to peddle bullshit.

"Some believed that the entire company was actually some sort of hoax." I'm going to translate that into what the author is really saying: "I would like to apologize for suggesting, as I did in one of my previous articles, on the basis of zero information, that botObjects was a hoax, when clearly it isn't. As Teri Hatcher put it in that great old episode of *Seinfeld*, 'They're real and they're spectacular!'"

"Some began thinking that botObjects was merely taking preorders, in order to run off with the money, while not actually working on manufacturing a product at all." = "*Mea culpa* for propagating the false rumor that they were going to take the money and run when it was a simple case of demand exceeding supply."

"Today comes news that will surprise even supporters of botObjects, and will certainly prove the company's naysayers wrong." = "I got it so so wrong!"

I should probably mention that we are widely known as "the controversial botObjects." But you know what: I reckon on the whole it's better to be controversial than not. If I recall, Dante's Inferno reserves a particularly harrowing fate for non-controversial types, the gray men who are neither loved nor hated. We had our fair share of love and hate, so I think we are safe (for now).

I really enjoyed the headline: "Not a Hoax After All". Which says it all, really.

"What do you think about this incredible turn of events for botObjects?" asks the Voice of 3D printing in his sign-off line. Well, what do you think? You can choose between (a) "They totally earned it—respect to them"; (b) "Daylight robbery!"; and (c) "Lock 'em up!"

I'll give you a clue: we weren't the ones getting pursued by the law.

52

AFTER THE END

The strategic fit is like thinking about the decision to marry. (The Professor)

It should have been the fairy-tale ending.

Just for a moment, set aside all the hullabaloo and the swirling rumor and the backstabbing: It's just a fact—we had the best thing on the market, of its kind. Second indisputable fact: Despite Gary's factory, we just didn't have the production facilities for a mass market product. So the union of botObjects and Mimetics3D should have been the perfect synthesis, a blissful coalition between our brains and their brawn. The ProDesk3D would never die, it would live on, resurrected and rectified, floating on a cloud of capital injections from a bigger and extremely benevolent company.

According to the Professor, "The strategic fit is like thinking about the decision to marry—between the acquirer and the startup."

And they lived happily ever after . . .

Only it didn't quite work out like that.

I love theory. But let us return to the brutal realm of fact—and the acrimonious divorce. Tom had done his best—more than I had—to accommodate the new regime. We had quickly discovered that, in fact, Mimetics had even less experience than we did in the realm of consumer 3D printing. We, with all our faults, had actually been producing more printers than they did. Tom toiled night and day to achieve a workable integration between them and us. Our frame was better than their frame, lighter yet stronger. Their "slicing" software, purported to be "the best," was a joke: they didn't even bother to decelerate at the corners. They didn't care if they ended up with blobs. We were way ahead of them. We hated blobs. Then one day Riley told us to incorporate their chip into our cartridge. It was all about security, apparently, preventing third-party intrusion. Fair enough, but it required a level of inspiration and perspiration beyond anything we had previously attained, reconfiguring the circuit board, the chip reader, the encryption, the data, everything. Finally Tom cracked it. Mission accomplished. And then one of the crew happened to say, "Oh, that. The software was hacked a year ago. It's all over the internet now." Nobody had informed Riley. They were too scared to mention it. Everything we had worked on for months proved to be a total waste of time and energy and expenditure. And, typically, Riley didn't really know what was happening at the sharp end. At the same time, Tom had been quietly starting to piece together a revolutionary machine that would be multi-material as well as multicolor. We would be able to print flexible, more complex objects. That was the dream. Another quantum leap.

And then in March 2015, I was fired and booted out of the building, with Tom following behind.

Six months later, on October 29, 2015, Riley Griffin resigned from Mimetics3D. His place was taken on an interim basis by our old friend, legal eagle John Thompson. Did Riley jump or was he pushed? Was Thompson the assassin? What we know for sure is that Riley exited pursued by lawsuits. Mimetics3D's own shareholders were in revolt, accusing Riley and the company of overestimating their ability to produce printers—exaggerating supply rather than demand—and thereby artificially inflating the share price. Without wanting to kick a guy when he's down, I reckon they definitely had a case. In reality, Mimetics3D was a corner shop, a Ma and Pa store, when it needed to be a Walmart. Was Riley guilty of making "false and misleading statements" (as one class action alleged)? You could make a case that he was being sued for acquiring botObjects—among so many other companies. Too many for him to be able to integrate them fully and profitably into the Mimetics3D system. He was brought down by his "buy, buy, buy" mentality. But, then again, he was probably laughing all the way to the bank.

In October, after the publication of their Q3 results, even Riley was forced to admit that "we failed to fully capitalize on the robust demand for our direct metal and consumer products." Their estimated revenues were cut by $50–90 million. The harsh reality is that the share price fell down a deep, dark hole, dragging shareholders down with it. At its height in 2014, a share in Mimetics3D was worth nearly $100. In 2015 that same share had slumped to around $10. That's worse than Bitcoin, and they call that volatile. If we'd taken our $50 million in Mimetics3D shares, as Riley first suggested, they would have been worth $5 million. If you invested in Mimetics3D in its golden age, under Riley, you have a right to feel ripped off and pissed off.

It's fair to say that after all the shots had been fired and the smoke cleared, the bottom had fallen out of the 3D printer market. As much through luck as good judgment, we had got into the market at just the right time and got out again when it was already on the slide and before it crashed through the floor. Mimetics3D saved us perhaps at the expense of sinking themselves.

Toward the end of 2015, shortly after Riley Griffin's departure, they drafted in an executive from Hewlett-Packard to take the helm. About the first thing he did was to cull the whole consumer division, for the simple reason that it wasn't making enough money. In other words, he killed the CubePro—which is to say our dear old ProDesk3D. The dream was dead. The hot tub bubble had definitively burst.

And I'm a reformed guy: I've given up smoking. There will be no more cigars in the hot tub. No more humidors in the office. No more cancer anxiety. I took that "No smoking in the building" line to heart.

Maybe it's not so surprising, after all the heart-stopping moments and the crises and the neuroses and the flaky robots, the mind-blowing highs and the soul-searing lows, the risks of death and disaster, that Tom's hair has turned several shades whiter than it used to be or that his next project was setting up an AI-powered mental health app, designed to comply with the "Health and Safety at Work Act," and boasting an instant "wellness checker." He reckoned it would cut the number of stress-related suicides. The last time I spoke to him he was wearing a kaftan and practicing meditation and had just returned from a week communing with Deepak Chopra somewhere on the West Coast. We both needed therapy—I guess this book is mine.

53

THE HOLY GRAIL

A heroic quest for the unattainable

All in all, you'd have to call it a happy ending. The Professor, in his rather abstract way, would call a "liquidity event." I've got a better name for it: the "Holy Grail Exit." Of course Tom and I were the major beneficiaries. But everyone involved received a share of the spoils on account of their heroic efforts. And I don't use the term "hero" lightly. Each of them performed an epic task and has gone on to achieve other great things.

Gaston Bachelier, Monsieur Firmware, keeps threatening to go back to his home country. But the reality is that he feels a thousand times more French by virtue of living in the United States than if he went back to Canada or even shipped off to France. He is not more Americanized; almost the opposite. His accent is more emphatically Maurice Chevalier or Charles Aznavour (or possibly ice hockey) than ever. He also keeps on intending to return to his open-source origins, but finds himself diverted by offers from the more "closed" alternatives, mainly because they pay much better. I don't blame him a bit. The last time I saw him he was playing double bass one night at

Smoke up on 106th Street and Broadway, his shirt hanging out of his pants.

Dylan Obeyesekere still has the ring through his nose. I'd be surprised if his verbal skills have improved that much. He has changed, but he's not that different. He has become obsessive about running and regularly enters marathons, both in London and New York. The last I heard he was planning to have a shot at an ultramarathon or one of those jaunts where you have to keep going for forty-eight hours at a stretch. It saves him the necessity of conversation. I mean, who has the strength for chitchat after you've run a couple of hundred miles?

Those guys are geniuses, almost godlike in my mind, without whose thousands of lines of code we would have been seriously stuffed. But I occasionally wonder if they ever found true love. Not that there is anything wrong with sublimation. We probably wouldn't have had botObjects without it. I believe that Eden Burberry, for one, has found happiness. She got married to her athletic girlfriend Tiffany. I know because they very nicely invited me to their wedding. They still go jogging together, but Eden has taught Tiffany to surf and their regular spot is out in the Hamptons on Long Island or up at Montauk. They keep going right through winter and don't seem to mind the freezing temperatures. Eden is tweeting for a big computer company these days.

I remain haunted by all the lunacy and the nightmare—sorry, the great adventure! the success story!—that was botObjects. And I have regrets. For example, I often think I shouldn't have asked Jack, the most sensitive of all of us, to take on the job of doorman or bouncer. You'd have to say he coped amazingly well, considering. He gave a whole different meaning to what the Professor calls "internal burn." I gather that he was more traumatized by his experience than any of us, but then he was on the receiving end of more vitriol than anyone else. I believe he has grown a big bushy beard and sailed off to a desert island somewhere and joined an obscure sect. I know he has vowed never to have anything to do with 3D printers ever again. Or me, for that matter. But maybe, when you weigh it all up, it was good for him. He has written a pilot for a television series about office life in a company that supposedly makes the most beautiful and functional vacuum cleaner ever, but never delivers on its promises. It's supposed to be a comedy. I don't know where he gets his ideas from.

I reckon the Professor is going to have to radically revise or possibly rip up the *Entrepreneur's Book of Secrets*. I need to go right back to the beginning and start again. But that's okay, I like starting over. In fact, I've got a new startup going, Autonomous Flight, which makes eVTOL aircraft—flying taxis. And I'm still working on Flixpremiere. I think there is a Syrian expression: one door closes and a thousand doors open—that's what I feel like.

Tom, like me, is impossible to pin down. He now has his own personal robot that serves him drinks and snacks and can answer his questions too, a combination of Rofi and Alexa. He has got rid of the legs completely: it may be the first skateboarding robot. He has about ten different startups on the go, too, mostly involving Web3, NFTs, and the Oculus headset. I remember when he first started talking about setting up an online mental health platform—on our all-time killer road trip. He was obviously inspired by my driving—combined with a perilously close encounter with the natives. You could say that the whole botObjects journey was like the worst road trip in the world, but one in which we returned richer rather than completely broke and broken. But I guess you also could call it a quest for the Holy Grail.

Oddly enough I happen to know quite a bit about the Holy Grail, or at least enough to know that no one knows anything about it. Many years ago I read *Holy Blood, Holy Grail*—the book that Dan Brown drew on for his *Da Vinci Code* thriller (while declining to pay for the privilege). The gist of it is that Jesus and Mary Magdalene got married and had kids and the "grail" is not a cup (whether a glorious, golden goblet or just a boring old beaker) that once contained the blood of Christ but in fact their bloodline carefully nurtured and preserved and prolonged into the present thanks to the mysterious Priory of Sion, with subplots involving the Templars and the royal family of France.

It was a great story, and the fact that it was more story—or conspiracy theory—than history did not deter me from turning it into a film script that earned me a small fortune and never got made. I always said Harvey Weinstein was a scoundrel, even then. But the notion of the Grail, or at least the pursuit thereof, has stayed with me.

I've long had a soft spot for that immortal image of the great knights of the Round Table riding out from Camelot in search of the sacred. That's what botObjects was, in essence: another quest—for the Holy Grail of 3D printing. I think we came pretty damn close—so tantalizingly close, in fact, that we were driven to the point of insanity. Everyone who worked for botObjects had their own version of this madcap pursuit of a dream.

And isn't that what entrepreneurship is after all? It's not all about profit or productivity; it's more a heroic quest for the unattainable. Most of the knights don't make it. But it's still good to get on your horse.

Talking of all the old botObjects crew: I haven't seen the Terminator in recent days, but I believe that he is even now plotting and planning his shot at the presidency.

54

YOU CAN'T MAKE IT UP

In the long run we are all dead

If you don't believe any of this story, I wouldn't blame you: I can scarcely believe it myself and I was there. I don't think I really believed we had sold the company until the moment I saw the payment land in my bank account. And I knew I wasn't dreaming right then because the final figure was minus the all-too-real legal fees; it wasn't some glorious round number. So in that respect, "$50 million" is a little bit of a fiction. Apart from that minor technicality, I think I can say of everything in this book, no matter how incredible, it is what it is. It only feels like a fantasy, a fever dream, part nightmare, part psychedelic hallucination.

Only, I should add, without sampling any actual LSD. I am not Jordan Belfort: I hope it won't be too much of a letdown if I state for the record that there were no orgies at botObjects, no industrial consumption of recreational drugs—we just didn't have time for it. So far as I can remember, there was no actual recreation during our 3D printer revolution (nor, by the same token, was there any need for rehab). Foosball was our limit. No day of corporate team bonding fun, shooting lasers or paintballs at one another. At the same time we experienced the kind of highs (together with a few memorable lows) that you are not going to get any other way. From the pink whistle all the way through to the pink watch, it was like treading a tightrope strung across Niagara. At any point along the way we could have made a misstep and fallen off, and it was a bloody long way down. I cringe now when I think of the stupid risks we were taking. We would have had to return all the money and we would probably be bankrupt. It would have been lawsuit heaven. Maybe we could have ended up in prison, doing time for offenses against reality. We would have been pariahs.

I have probably used the word "I" about one thousand times in this book—and there's a couple more for good measure—but to tell the truth, it feels to me now like that must have been some other guy. I would never have done any of that, not in my right mind. Maybe he had serious mental health issues. What was that dude even thinking of, in the hot tub, smoking a cigar and conjuring up a nonexistent 3D printer that would surpass every other 3D printer? You and your hobbyist friend, you're going to what? Print out a rather wobbly robot and shove him in front of the cameras on Fox television? No way! Man, are you crazy?

You thought this was going to be *the next biggest thing*? You thought it was going to blow away Microsoft and Amazon? That was a certain sign of madness. But for almost a year and half that's exactly what we did think. It was better than the Mona Lisa (according to the guy in Perth). We thought our little machine was going to change the world. It was going to be bigger than Apple, bigger than the internet. We were going to be billionaires, not mere millionaires.

We were, it will be said, unrealistic. As it is, I can't go and buy my own private island in the South Pacific. I can't buy Chelsea FC outright. I am not an oligarch. It's not too frustrating, but I just wanted to register the point that nothing ever quite measures up to the dream, least of all when 3D printed. It could have been a lot better, but it could also have been a helluva lot worse. I often wonder what could have happened if we had given Mimetics3D the cold shoulder and instead taken the fifteen and a half million of private investment and run with it. We could still be busting a gut to make and sell 3D printers every day. Maybe we would be world-leaders. Maybe not. On the whole, I'm glad we got out—but I'm very glad we got in.

Something Tom said after it was all over and we were walking away: "Don't make me do this again! It was too difficult." It's true, we took something complicated and made it even more complicated. Three motors weren't enough—it had to have twelve. It's like a car that can go at 100 mph and you say, why don't we make it go 300 mph (ideally, without crashing)? And Tom and I knew next to nothing about cars.

But, then again, it wasn't totally insane. As a general rule, without risk there is no reward. And we had a good team. Tom was already good on software, but how do you make the transition to hardware? Answer: you hire the people who can fill in the gaps.

We hired the experts, people like Gaston and Dylan, to sort out the software and the firmware. We brought in Gary, who proved that our vision was real. They would all go home every night thinking about how to solve one problem or another—or several. And wake up the next day and fix it.

From the moment we got out of the hot tub, we wanted to be world leaders. As I said to Tom, you're either all in or you're all out. In the end, against the odds, we managed to invent something beautiful and (on a good day) functional. Sticking Rofi on Fox Business was nuts, but on the other hand it got us on the front page of a trade magazine. We had distributors from around the world beating a path to our door.

The ProDesk3D was a dream machine, premised on the existence of a mass market. We thought there would be millions of people making the things that they needed. It could have been perfect for a pandemic—you need never go shopping again! We made many things, it is true: a pair of glasses, vases, a watch, a recorder, a Daft Punk–style helmet, an iPhone case. But the sad truth was that they were all relatively low-grade, they were clunky, they were brittle. In a word, they were tchotchkes, pointless ephemera. And it took way too long to make them. If you want to pop out a frying pan or an ashtray or a pair of shoes, you want to do it in ten minutes, not three hours. Ours was the fastest printer out there, but it still needed to be ten times faster. I wanted our printer to be functional—and have perfect form. But we learned that you couldn't have both. For higher quality and greater speed, you need to get seriously industrial. We were right back where we started, in other words, with a printer the size of Tom's garage. We had taken the printer out of the factory and put it within reach of everyone's home—and now it has gone back to the factory after all.

We had our day in the sun, we had a season, we had at least a first birthday: and then we died, but then all companies must die. As John Maynard Keynes wisely observed, "In the long run we are all dead." Ninety-nine percent of all companies in the history of the world are no longer with us. Amazon will die, Apple will die, Microsoft will die. Even Beretta, which has been selling us weapons since the Renaissance, is ultimately doomed. Perhaps capitalism itself will expire at long last. It's just a matter of time. Great empires rise and fall. So too, in its ultra-slim, turbocharged, rock 'n roll, rocky, aluminized, fast-forward fashion, botObjects. New formations will arise in their place. I like to imagine that, a hundred thousand years from now, a roaming archaeologist of the future will happen to dig up some of our greatest creations and will find himself puzzling over the evidence of the zenith of our own civilization, as manifested by the botObjects set of transparent dentures made out of crystal polymer. Or a robot that can't walk. And they will marvel at this new Tutankhamun, these myriad terra-cotta soldiers, and scratch their heads over the great mystery. Perhaps some young intern digger will utter the magic words, "Awesome, dude!"

EPILOGUE

The future is here.

Did everyone want to be a maker? No, they didn't. A 3D printer is not for everyone, only for a subset of people who want to create objects. There are the serious geeks who want to do this at home or in the garage. I salute them. They are exceptional human beings, but we didn't want exceptional, we wanted ordinary, everyday citizens. The 3D printer business wasn't a bubble (it didn't burst), but it was driven in part by a hype cycle: take a look at the share prices, and after the meteoric rise and catastrophic fall you'll see we're now well past the "trough of disillusionment" and are on the verge of the sunlit uplands of the "plateau of productivity." I still get daily updates and alerts in my inbox from the 3D industry. The technical advances over the last few years have been sensational. Printers are more reliable and versatile. We are printing whole houses, bridges, body parts, cars, space rockets, and robots (more reliable successors to Rofi). The next Aston Martin is going to be printed (Porsche and Bugatti likewise). The serious 3D printer is perfect if you're a designer or you want to make prototypes or small components. But it's not like you're switching on the microwave or clicking on an app. These days 3D printing is more sustainable too: you use recycled plastic, bottles from the beach, cornstarch, or soy. 3D is going plant-based. You can buy 3D printed, vegan-friendly, sustainable salmon, for example (no, I haven't tested it).

And it's salmon-pink too, with a color gradient. In the post botObjects world, full color is standard. I think I can say, hand on heart, that we changed the history of 3D printing. It's become part of everyday life, just as we expected. One day there will be a 3D printer the size of a coffee-maker. Tell me I'm wrong.

"THE FUTURE IS HERE" was a tagline from one of our commercials. With hindsight, it would have been more precise to say, "THE FUTURE ISN'T QUITE HERE YET" (not a line that was going to pull in the punters). Ten years from now, everything we said a few years ago will turn out to be true. Reality is still catching up. We were just way ahead of our time. We were born too soon. But there is life after death. Increasingly I find myself identifying with Alec Guinness, Obi-Wan Kenobi, after that brush with Darth Vader's light saber: "If you strike me down, I'll become more powerful than you can possibly imagine." On second thought, maybe that is a bit too Force-ful, but you get the general idea.

Every company is different. Just as practically every game of chess is unique (Claude Shannon reckoned that there are 10^{120} possible games—more than there are stars in the universe), the history of our startup is unlike any other. It can never be repeated, in just this way, with precisely this cast of characters, not in the entire future history of the universe. But some of the moves will be familiar all the same, and especially the missteps and mistakes. Maybe we made more than our fair share of blunders. Maybe our heroic dreams and fabulous ambitions could not help but collide with the reality principle. Either way someone will learn from the sparks flying up. I've always wanted to get to the bottom of how business works and get to do it better. I like to think that the science of entrepreneurship has been advanced by our mad experiment. One day all our experiences will be digitized and rolled up into one immense algorithm that will map out new worlds and enable young adventurers to boldly go. The saga of botObjects will thereby imprint itself, in full color, on enterprises that are yet to come.

One day I may have to pass on the baton to Theo, our (then) fifteen-year-old intern/trainee, now in his mid-twenties and setting the world on fire. Although that is perhaps an unfortunate metaphor in his case. He told me that he had been inspired by his dose of work experience at botObjects to make a prosthetic arm for his high school science project. It was known as the "arm muscle booster" or, more popularly, the "robo arm." If you've seen the climactic scene in *Aliens* where Ripley dons an exosuit cargo-loader to grapple with the otherwise unstoppable alien and finally chuck it out of the spaceship, you'll understand what it was all about. On a smaller scale, Theo was aiming not to replace your arm but to enhance your normal strength, to turn you into a little bit of a superman/woman with the addition of an apparatus, hinged at the elbow, powered by a small motor on your back and a controller in your left hand. And—this was his point—it was all produced with the use of a ProDesk3D. I felt a distinct sense of pride that the younger generation had adopted our tech. Over an entire semester, often working until 3 a.m., Theo painstakingly printed all the parts required to make his turbocharged arm. When fully assembled it worked a treat. Theo could lift weights at least twice as heavy as he could normally manage. He was a slim lad who had been turned into a regular Schwarzenegger. Then he brought all his kit into school on the day of the demonstration. So far so good. I should have asked him to stop the story right there.

Theo made the elementary mistake of leaving his backpack, unzipped at the top with a spaghetti of wires tumbling out of it, in the principal's office. When the principal's secretary spotted it, she assumed it must be a bomb (those darn kids were bound to have it in for the principal, weren't they?) and naturally called in the bomb squad. Fortunately, our hero was able to get there in time and reassure everyone piled up outside the office that it was not a bomb but only his robo arm. Relief all round. They called off the bomb squad. And then Theo's backpack exploded (the electrics short-circuited, so maybe you can't blame botObjects for once) and the place filled with smoke. So the entire school had to be evacuated anyway. No one was hurt. But Theo's robo arm was never quite the same afterward. Ah well, all part of the enduring legacy of botObjects. No great progress was ever achieved without significant disruption.

You can't buy a ProDesk3D anymore. But at least we donated our little printer to a science museum in the hope of keeping the revolutionary printer alive or of some use for generations to come. Maybe, right now, a bunch of schoolkids are looking at it. Maybe they're also getting inspired by what we did. Unreal! they may say. Maybe, on the other hand, with the wisdom of youth, they're saying—that was mad! Ridiculous! Naive! They were fools! I'm okay with that.

BIBLIOGRAPHY

Books

Jordan Belfort, *Wolf of Wall Street* (Bantam, 2007).

Phil Knight, *Shoe Dog: a Memoir by the Creator of Nike* (Simon & Schuster, 2016).

Michael Lewis, *The Big Short: Inside the Doomsday Machine* (Simon & Schuster, 2010).

Howard Schultz, *Pour Your Heart Into It: How Starbucks Built a Company One Cup at a Time* (Hachette, 1999).

Online Periodicals

CNET.com

solidsmack.com

TechCrunch.com

3Dprint.com

T3 magazine

Websites

Joris Peel, VoxelFab.com

Martin Warner, entrepreneurseminar.com

ACKNOWLEDGMENTS

My respect and gratitude to all the amazing team at botObjects—and our partners—who came on the journey with me. With a particular shout-out to techno genius Mike Duma, my cofounder and friend. And apologies to anyone who ended up on the cutting room floor.